PSYCH UP
OR
PSYCH OUT

THE SPORT PARENT'S GUIDE TO HELPING YOUNG ATHLETES MASTER MENTAL TOUGHNESS IN SPORT

BY

MICHAEL J. ASKEN, PH.D.
AND
BRETON M. ASKEN

PSYCH UP OR PSYCH OUT

FIRST SUNBURY PRESS EDITION
Printed in the United States of America
November 2011

ISBN 978-1-934597-76-7

Published by:
Sunbury Press, Inc.
2200 Market Street
Camp Hill, PA   17011

www.sunburypress.com

Camp Hill, Pennsylvania   USA

TABLE OF CONTENTS

For the sake of editorial economy, we will now alternate the gender of the pronouns we use by chapter. Obviously whether we are using "he" or "she," the information applies equally well to both male and female athletes, unless otherwise noted.

FOREWORD

It is my pleasure to introduce this book, Psych Up or Psych Out: The Sport Parent's Guide to Helping Young Athletes Master Mental Toughness in Sport. Dr. Michael Asken and Breton Asken have put together a collection of concepts and skills which taken together discuss the sport psychology and "mental toughness" required to excel in sport.

The book begins with a personal experience from Breton's high school sports career where he describes his use of performance-enhancing mental imagery; providing an extremely good example of how it aids performance in critical and difficult situations. It also uniquely and strikingly bonds one author to the other, much in the same way the book seeks to bond you as a sport parent to your young athlete through understanding and developing the psychological skills of mental toughness for sports performance.

The information in the book is presented in an effective manner much akin to a coach preparing a game plan. The approach allows parents and athletes to understand and apply the concepts and skills to all sports and make adaptations for a specific sport of interest.

The essential relationships between physical and psychological conditioning, or as it is also described, between mind and body, and how a strong connection between the two is paramount to a well-prepared athlete are very well presented. Multiple quotations by various elite athletes and coaches are inspiring and validate the importance of the psychological game as seen in mental toughness for success in sport competition.

The skills described such as goal setting, concentration skills, performance-enhancing imagery and optimal performance state development are important for athletes of all ages and not just for sport, but for life challenges, as well.

As a team physician for the past 35-40 years, I have utilized psychology in training and in evaluating athletes. I have seen athletes attempting to "put it all together," that is, combine physical skill with mental toughness. That is not as easy at it might seem. However, Psych Up or Psych Out provides the best in how to do this, in the most appropriate manner and in a way that helps you and your athlete promote total sports development together.

As sports medicine physicians, we like to think we have all the answers, at least for the physiologic aspects of sport. We can now do pretty well, but as sport psychology progresses, we find there is a lot more to know about the interaction of the mind and body in sport. The same is true for sport parents and young athletes. There is a lot more you can know about mental toughness and performance from a balanced and scientific perspective. This is an extremely enjoyable book, reads well and offers us all this opportunity to learn more and enhance enjoyment and performance in sport… and life.

Michael Cordas, D.O.,
Fellow, American Osteopathic Academy of Sports Medicine
Fellow, American Academy of Family Physicians
Director, Primary Care Sports Medicine Fellowship Program
Pinnacle Health Care System
Harrisburg, Pennsylvania

IT WORKS!

Rewind to the summer of 1998. I'm eight years old, and after three years of playing recreation level soccer, I am about to start my first season on a travel team. Despite my youth, I understand that this is the type of soccer that actually "means something," and it was time to catch up to my older brother's trophy and medal collection. It is the eve of my first game, and it just happens to be the start of a weekend of tournament play, which is a perfect opportunity to start my own hardware collection. I'm in my motel room having about as much success sleeping, as an insomniac sipping on Mountain Dew.

Sensing my restlessness from the bed next to mine, my dad, a sport psychologist, offers his wisdom. (Looking back, I suspect this was very exciting for him to finally have an opportunity to impart his expertise on the *mental* side of the game. My athleticism had not come from him (sorry, Dad), but this is where he could contribute to my development. He tells me to close my eyes, and picture myself in the game tomorrow. Envision the passes I would make, the shots I would take, and the players I would defend. Pay attention to the feel of the ball, and the slickness of the grass from the morning dew. I struggled with this, but I continued to try until eventually I fell asleep.

I would use this mental imagery technique again and again as I grew up, realizing quickly, that just like any skill, I needed to practice if I wanted to improve and make it useful. Over the years I found myself mentally prepared for big games and situations, and also avoided many sleepless nights.

Fast-forward to the fall of 2008. Fourteen years of soccer under my belt, including the past three at the varsity high school level and I am entering my senior year as a team captain. After toying with the idea since about seventh grade, I finally went out to be the kicker for our football team. As it turned out, the team was in desperate need of a kicker and my soccer skills translated in such a way that kicking came naturally to me. Soccer being my first commitment, I practiced with the football team all of ten minutes per week. I would occasionally practice on my own, but I relied predominantly on the "foot-eye" coordination from soccer to be enough.

My first football game of the year, and the first home game of the year, came against the team that ended our previous season by beating us in the District Title game. Instead of being nervous, I found myself excited and prepared. I know that was because the previous couple of nights, just like ten years before, I had fallen asleep envisioning myself in my stance, awaiting the snaps, seeing the holds, and kicking the ball (sometimes my mental football was replaced by a soccer ball- but like I said, it takes practice).

My first two kicks were extra points that went through without issue, just like they had in my mind many times before, but my composure would be tested further. The game wore on, and early in the 4th quarter the game was tied. I quickly begin realizing that this game could be decided by my making, or missing, a kick. I started to think it was a little too early in the season, and surely too early in my football career, for this kind of pressure. Sure enough, the game entered overtime. The rules are college-style, with alternating possessions, and I remember it this way.

We have the ball first. It's third down, and from where we are right now it will be around a 25-yard field goal; a glorified extra point in my mind. On that play our quarterback is sacked. Now it's a 33-yard field goal, but still well within my range. The stakes are now much different than they were during my extra points earlier in the game. Up until this point, my excitement had held the nerves back, though the nerves were picking up some momentum.
I trot onto the field and get into my stance, knowing that if I were to miss this kick the opponent would need only a field goal on their possession to win the game. The physical atmosphere in which I found myself was much different than most soccer games, but in my mental atmosphere the pressure of the many penalty kicks I had taken over the years was simply transformed to that of a field goal. The first time I had kicked a football, while wearing pads and a helmet rather than soccer shorts (a transition not very seamless the first time you do it), was roughly two hours earlier during warm-ups. Now, in my first football game ever, the first game of the year, in front of our classmates and families, under the lights, in overtime, the game essentially rested on the soccer cleat that housed my right foot.

False start…offense…5-yard penalty… still 4th down. Apparently aware of the rookie situation behind him, one of blockers jumps too soon in an attempt to make sure that I'd have all the time I need. Now a 38-yard field goal, but I told myself that I still know it's in my range. It was in my range in my performance imagery practice, even though my imagery guess of the feel of the pads and helmet had been less than accurate. The ball is snapped, the hold is down, step one, step two, kick. Right down the middle, just like when I was lying in bed the night before.

We didn't stop them on their possession, and we lost the game. Heartbreaking finish aside, the pressure-filled situation in which I found myself would generally be considered insurmountable for someone with my football credentials. What set me apart was the fact that even though I had never kicked in a football game, I had split the uprights over and over again, before my kicks in practice, when preparing pre-game, and on the sidelines as I prepared to answer the call.

I had learned how important and powerful sport psychology mental toughness techniques were to my performance in athletics and, now, in life. It was kind of nice that it was my dad who had helped me discover this. That is why I am so pleased to be part of this book and to help you, as parents, help your athlete discover the importance of the mental game.

- **Breton M. Asken**
Chapel Hill, North Carolina 2011

INTRODUCTION

The following sentence is the most powerful all-encompassing affirmation I can make for sport psychology: Your mental approach to conditioning and competing (which is sport psychology) determines how much you learn from your participation, the amount of enjoyment you experience, the number of years you will maintain interest, and your place on the results page. All athletic consequences are highly dependent on mental attributes.

> -Lyle Nelson, Three-time Olympian
> U.S. Biathalon Team
> Winner, NBC TV's Survival of the Fittest

If you have a son or daughter who is a young athlete, you already know, or will soon know, that you are engaged in one of the most wonderful experiences of parenthood. Being the parent of a young and developing athlete can bring unsurpassed joy and excitement. It also brings significant responsibility.

> **I don't believe professional athletes should be role models.**
> **I believe parents should be role models....**
>
> **-Charles Barkley**
> NBA MVP and Hall of Fame
> 11-time NBA All-Star

As a youth sport parent you want your athlete (and hopefully other athletes, as well) to have the very best of the positive potential that sports can offer. It is no secret that youth sports can fall short of this promise. They can be a stressful, negative, or harmful experience if they are poorly planned, unwisely trained, or are void of positive parental awareness and involvement. But that is a topic and discussion for another time, and is addressed elsewhere by Martens (1978) *Joy and Sadness in Children's Sports*, Murphy (1999) *The Cheers and the Tears*, Ryan (2000) *Little Girls in Pretty Boxes* and Sperber (2001) *Beer and Circus*. The good news is that such bad news can be avoided.

Youth sport is a formative and experience-filled intense emotional and psychological engagement for both athletes and parents. In that emotion is much of the promise and problem, the essence and excess of youth sports' impact. It is the understanding, training and mastery of the psychology and emotion of sport that will, to a great degree, define the quality of the experience for you and your athlete. In addition to talent and skill, it is the emotional component that paves the road to excellence in development of performance and sustained success.

This book will help you begin to understand the concepts and techniques that lead to effective psychological skills that can maximize motivation, performance and enjoyment of competition. This is a set of skills that is commonly called "mental toughness." While there is much more to mental toughness than can be described here, this book will help you to assess whether your young athlete's training is providing exposure to and development in effective and healthy aspects of mental toughness. It will also help you to promote and reinforce healthy aspects of mental toughness. We will discuss the vague concept called mental toughness, why it is needed, why it needs to be trained (and why it is often not), and how it can be trained.

Youth sports are a complex undertaking – organizationally, financially, socially, emotionally and psychologically. We will focus on just one aspect, a crucial one to be sure, but just one aspect of the competitive youth sports experience. We will assume that other factors in the foundation for a healthy and successful youth sports experience are in place.

> **Winning is fun and it's the American way.**
> **But for kids at a young age, athletics should**
> **be stressed for the pleasure of participating.**
>
> **- Roger Staubach**
> "Captain Comeback"
> Dallas Cowboys Quarterback
> Super Bowl MVP & Hall of Fame

We will assume that as youth sport parents you have assured, to the best of your ability, that your athlete has access to a program built on sportsmanship and competent developmentally-focused coaching.

We will assume that as youth sports parents you value goals such as the unique opportunity to bond with your young athlete, to fill leisure time with a safe and productive activity, to develop health and fitness, to train talent and develop skills, and to promote personal and interpersonal development, discipline, and respect for effort and achievement in oneself and others.

> **The role of my parents was perfect. They were helpful**
> **but never interfered with my tennis….**
> **If they had told me I had to practice four hours a day**
> **and pushed it down my throat, I would have quit.**
>
> **- Bjorn Borg**
> 11 Grand Slam Titles
> 5 Consecutive Wimbledon Titles

We will assume that absent are problematic parental motivations such as over-identification with your athlete in a vain and ill-fated search for glory, selfish over-investment in a quest for financial and/or social status returns or parental competition (not just "keeping up with the Joneses," but beating them).

4

We will also assume that you want to give your young athlete every opportunity to maximize his or her potential. By attending to the psychological and emotional components of competition – mental toughness – you are giving your athlete the best opportunity to truly become the *complete athlete*. Parents, though often maligned in youth sports, are rarely thanked enough for their efforts and, indeed, the sacrifices they lovingly make for their young athletes. Let us thank you right now for caring enough to give your athlete the full set of equipment to achieve excellence in his or her sport and life.

> **Sport is where an entire life can be compressed into a few hours, where the emotions of a lifetime can be felt on an acre or two of ground, where a person can suffer and die and rise again on six miles of trails through a New York City park. Sport is a theater where sinner can turn saint and a common man become an uncommon hero, where the past and the future can fuse with the present. Sport is singularly able to give us peak experiences where we feel completely one with the world and transcend all conflicts as we finally become our own potential.**
>
> **- George A. Sheehan, M.D.**
> The "Running Doctor"

I

THE MENTAL GAME PLAN

For all the concrete assets that a world-level championship effort demands – strategy and training and functional necessities – very often the decisive quality is ethereal. It floats through the neuro synapses of what scientists call a brain, but the more spiritual among us would call the mind.

-David Jones, Sportswriter

WHY SPORT PSYCHOLOGY and MENTAL TOUGHNESS ARE ESSENTIAL IN COMPETITION

Have you ever really stopped to think about how important mental preparation and mental toughness are for excelling in sports?

Just think about all the terms that are used to describe an athlete's readiness to compete. They are almost always related to the athlete's psychology. Athletes talk about being **PSYCHED UP** or being **INTO IT** or **READY TO GO** or being **UP FOR IT.**

Can you or your athlete think of other terms that are used in sport to describe mental readiness, mental toughness, and motivation to compete? Have your athlete write them in the spaces provided. Some other examples are provided later.

TERMS FOR MENTAL TOUGHNESS
AND
PSYCHOLOGICAL READINESS TO COMPETE

_____

_____

_____

_____

_____

_____

Also, did you ever listen carefully to reasons (or excuses) that are given as to why an athlete or team did not perform well? Don't you hear things like:

We weren't hungry enough …
We lost our momentum …
She wasn't focused …
He didn't want it badly enough …
It was mental mistakes …
We took them for granted …
We didn't come to play …

Notice these are all psychological reasons that imply that a team or athlete was not mentally prepared for the challenge. And, while such psychological reasons are often given for losing, psychological skills, as well, like mental readiness and mental toughness, are the keys to succeeding and winning. The problem is that the psychological skills needed for maximum performance are too often assumed, or ignored, until there is a poor result.

We were lucky enough to know and work with one of the great indoor pro soccer goalies of all time, Scoop Stanisic. As an elite professional goalkeeper, Scoop was well aware of the importance of psychological skill for success. He said it this way:

When talent meets talent
When hard work is matched
Against hard work
Only mental toughness can give you an edge.

Almost every great athlete and coach will agree that mental toughness is essential in order to truly excel in performance. The great baseball player Willie Mays summed it up this way:

What you're thinking, what shape your mind is in,
Is what makes the biggest difference of all.

Athletes are very respectful of the power of mental toughness, and of athletes (even opponents) who demonstrate it. World-class tennis player Rafael Nadal was recently asked, "If you could play against any player in history, who would it be?" He replied:

I'd Choose (Bjorn) Borg. He had such an incredible Mental Approach to the Game.
He Had Ice in his veins and I'd love to see what I could do Against Him.

So what is mental toughness? There are many different ideas about what constitutes mental toughness. Sometimes mental toughness is said to be having "the right stuff" or "the intangibles," and some people believe either you have it or you don't, even as a young athlete. Some people think it is about being aggressive or even violent. Some people think that mental toughness cannot be trained. All these people are wrong. Mental toughness can be broken down in a way to better understand it, and to help develop it effectively.

We define Mental Toughness this way:

Mental toughness is understanding, possessing, and being able to use a set of psychological skills that allow for effective, and even maximal execution, flexibility and adaptability in performance, and importantly, persistence of effort and skills that have been developed by coaching, practice and experience. Mental toughness expresses itself every day, but especially in highly challenging situations.

It should be noted that mental toughness is not necessarily about aggression in sport. It is about a set of positive psychological performance skills that promote competitive skill excellence and persistence. It is about a set of skills that can be trained and improved in any athlete.

As an athlete moves to higher and higher levels of competition, mental toughness becomes more and more important. It is often quoted that at elite levels of performance, success is 90% mental. (Yogi Berra said baseball is 90% mental and the other half is physical !)

Why is this? The answer is rather simple. At elite levels of competition, all athletes have the physical attributes and skills to perform well, or they wouldn't be there. Therefore, the difference is the mental game, or who has the mental toughness to work the hardest, concentrate most intensely, bounce back, and stay staunch in the face of setbacks.

Extreme skier Reggie Christ put it this way:

It's amazing how much of this is mental.
Everybody's in good shape.
Everybody knows how to ski.
Everybody has good equipment...

A major characteristic of superior performers, compared to that of more average competitors, is the ability to perform at a high level *consistently*, not just have a great play here and there. Once again, Willie Mays had some valuable insight into what makes a great athlete. He said:

It isn't hard to be good from time to time in sports.
What's tough is being good every day.

Mental toughness and consistency in performance are a little different at youth and developmental levels of sport. A lack of consistency is to be expected, as this is part of developing. Certainly, you will come to see a great frustration for coaches and, perhaps you as a parent, with inconsistent performance by the team and your athlete. It is frustrating to see excellent and even amazing effort and skill one day, and what seems to be a complete collapse at the next competition. But this is the nature of youth sport.

Consistency is also a valued goal, but great frustration, at the highest levels of competition. It is captured in the rhetorical question of frustrated fans when they ask "which team is going to show up today to play?" And the need for, and value of, consistency occurs much earlier these days even in youth sports, as soon as developmental and instructional levels are passed. Consistency should be stressed as a goal and value; increasing consistency should be expected as a sign of progress, but some inconsistency should also be accepted as part of development.

Mental toughness may have less of an impact at the very basic levels of youth sport. At younger ages there will be a greater disparity in physical development, maturity and skill, which may account for differences in quality of performance. As parents, it is important to recognize that, just as with physical training, it is critical to differentiate the reality of sport at the recreational level, versus sport at the competitive level. Nonetheless, even the earliest developmental phases are an appropriate time to begin working on those psychological skills of mental toughness, which are so crucial as competition increases. Furthermore, beginning to master mental toughness, even at lower levels of competition and in rudimentary or age appropriate ways, will help maximize a young athlete's performance, motivation, and enjoyment, within the limits of his or her physical gifts and maturity.

Other terms for Mental Toughness include:

- **The Inner Game**
  - **The Mental Edge**
    - **The Mental Advantage**
      - **Being Pumped**
        - **Being in the Zone**

WHY MENTAL TOUGHNESS IS NOT TRAINED CONSISTENTLY

We continue to be amazed at how many athletes and coaches have still not been exposed to scientifically based principles and skills of sport psychology and mental toughness. Even though most agree that success is anywhere from 50 to 90 percent "mental," little or no time is spent coaching or practicing psychological skills.

There are several reasons why this contradiction persists. A main one is the misconception that mental toughness cannot be developed (but try to tell that to the Army, Navy, Air Force, Marines or SEALs!). While there are individuals who are "naturally" mentally tough, or became so through various life experiences or their physiology, everyone can improve their psychological skills of mental toughness.

Another reason that mental toughness is ignored in coaching and training is the belief that it occurs naturally by just practicing or playing a lot. Mental toughness is believed to develop certainly and consistently as a result of skill training. Wrong.

Psychological performance skills need to be trained directly. No smart coach, athlete, or parent believes that optimal condition and endurance occurs from merely mastering a golf swing, or from good form in the starting blocks on a track. Specific muscle exercises, time in the weight room, and proper nutrition, need to occur in order to maximize the skill. Likewise, mental toughness cannot be expected to be a "side effect" of other training.

Yet another reason why sport psychology training does not occur is that coaches, athletes, and parents do not know how to train mental toughness skills. At worst, there are many misconceptions about training mental toughness. There may be a regression to use the model that was experienced in the military. (The reference above was not meant to suggest that military mental toughness training is the model for sport; in fact, the military has been questioning and changing the way they develop mental toughness). Or, there may be the mistaken belief that just telling an athlete to "relax" or "focus" or "get pumped" will lead to that result. Hopefully, no one believes that telling an athlete to "just put it in the basket" is the best way to instruct and develop free throw ability. But very often, we seem to believe that telling an athlete to relax will induce calmness.

Fortunately, these days there are more athletes and coaches who are aware of sport psychology (the science and not hearsay) techniques and approaches to maximize mental toughness. After reading this book, you will be among a select group of parents who have also become aware of how to help their athletes maximize potential and performance.

YOUR ROLE IN DEVELOPING SPORT PSYCHOLOGY SKILLS & MENTAL TOUGHNESS

Trying to tell you how to help develop sport psychology and mental toughness skills in your athlete is a bit like trying to tell you how to parent your son or daughter; it would be a bit presumptuous to do so. Clearly, everyone has different styles and perspectives, and much of how you bring the information in this book to your athlete depends upon the overall nature of the relationship that you have with your athlete.

> **What's important is that kids discover baseball is fun – and it gets more fun as you get better at it.**
>
> **- Mickey Mantle**
> New York Yankees center fielder
> 20-time All-Star, Hall of Fame
> 7-time World Series champion

The age of your athlete, his physical, mental and emotional maturity, motivation and other similar factors will also affect how to best present sport psychology mental toughness training. But let us make some general suggestions.

At a minimum, educate yourself about mental training in sport (this book is a good first step). Not only will this make you a better mental coach within your parenting role, but as important, it will allow you to assess how well your athlete's coach and training program are providing beneficial sport psychology training, if any at all. It may also allow you to advocate for this emphasis in the sports program, and monitor that pseudo-psychology is not being offered.

If your athlete is lucky enough to be in a program where coaching and training includes sport psychology and mental toughness training, you can support the coach in his or her efforts. You can reinforce what is being coached, and help your athlete gain these skills more quickly and effectively.

If you have a hands-on or even coaching type of relationship with your athlete, you can use this book to develop an introductory program for your son or daughter. It need not be a comprehensive program; you can contribute by helping to train or refine just a specific skill.

If you are not sports-wise or talented yourself, or if you don't have a directed/coaching relationship with your athlete, your contribution to his sport psychology knowledge can be more subtle. Look for windows of opportunity to pass on an idea or make a suggestion to stimulate your athlete's curiosity. Often times this may occur when there is a problem, like performance being less than expected overall, or that one game or competition that was disappointing and your athlete is looking for help and ideas. Certainly there will positive opportunities, as well.

Finally, as you become more aware of, and attuned to, sport psychology and mental toughness techniques, you are likely to see examples of them on TV or at other high level competitions or games. You will notice batters taking deep centering breaths before entering the box, weightlifters focusing before a lift, or skaters and gymnasts engaging in performance-enhancing mental imagery before their routine. You may read articles or interviews that highlight the psychology of elite athletes that reflect what you will learn in this book. Share these examples as a way to introduce sport psychology concepts, or to reinforce those that you have already covered. This is especially useful for a young athlete who may have a bias against "that psychological stuff" in sport or otherwise.

CURVEBALLS IN YOUR HELPING DEVELOP SPORT PSYCHOLOGY MENTAL TOUGHNESS

As wonderful, gratifying, and beneficial as helping your young athlete develop psychological sport skills and mental toughness can be, there are some curveballs, or pitfalls, of which you should be aware.

First, recognize that mental training and mental toughness are never a substitute for good coaching, practice, and physical conditioning. Psychological skills are essential and are what the military calls a "force multiplier." Successful athletes have both physical and psychological excellence. One is not more important than the other. The interactive and performance-enhancing contributions of each are like asking: In the following equation, $2 \times 3 = 6$, which is more important for the six, is it the two or the three?

Obviously, both are necessary in this instance. Both lead to the result, and neither is more important than the other. Make sure you include all the important components of developing a successful athlete, from physical conditioning to mental toughness.

Secondly, if you haven't learned this already, you are likely to find out at some point that, as in all things parental, kids often respond better to instruction and suggestions when they come from someone else. The very same advice shunned from you will be accepted as golden wisdom when offered by a coach, uncle, teacher, sibling, or sports commentator. This will depend on your overall relationship with your athlete and his view of your command of the sport. The point is to recognize that despite the good intentions, YOU may not be the best mental coach for your young athlete.

This leads to the third point which is that you should not become frustrated or irritated if your athlete doesn't welcome your mental coaching contributions, especially initially. This may reflect the overall relationship, or just a rejection of "that mental stuff" by your athlete. It does take a somewhat mature and experienced athlete to recognize the value of the mental game, and be able to relate to it.

Finally, as you will come to read in this book, every athlete is different. Mental toughness skills need to be defined and trained with an individual blueprint. Therefore, don't be surprised if the psychological game plan for other athletes in your child's program looks different from yours. And especially recognize the need for a unique and individualized approach if you have more than one young athlete in your family. Every athlete, like every youngster is different.

Curveballs can be tough, but if anticipated, they can be hit out of the park.

II

FUNDAMENTALS

I always felt that my greatest asset was not my physical ability, it was my mental ability.

-Bruce Jenner
Gold Medal Decathlon
Olympic and Pan American Games

PHYSICALLY STRONG AND MENTALLY TOUGH

It might seem strange to begin a book about *psychological* training with a discussion about *physical* conditioning. If you think about it, however, you will see that it makes perfect sense.

The mind and body are connected. They both function together, and they both affect each other. Everything we do or feel is controlled by our brain. The body is the environment in which the brain "lives and works." If you want your young athlete's brain and mind to be the best, you need to help her take care of her body and be in top physical shape.

Good physical conditioning is the basis for successful performance in every sport. Some of the reasons for this are obvious; some of the reasons may be less well-known. In the space below, go ahead and list the potential sport performance benefits of top physical conditioning of which you and your athlete are aware.

SPORT PERFORMANCE BENEFITS
OF TOP PHYSICAL CONDITIONING

_____

_____

_____

How many did you name? How many did your athlete name? And here's the key question: Did you or your athlete list any psychological and mental toughness benefits of physical conditioning, as well?

Important performance benefits of top physical conditioning for athletes are listed below.

> **INCREASED ENDURANCE**
> **INCREASED STRENGTH**
> **INCREASED FLEXIBILITY**
> **DECREASED SENSITIVITY TO PAIN**
> **DECREASED PHYSICAL REACTIONS TO STRESS**
> **DECREASED INJURY**
> **CLEARER THINKING & BETTER DECISIONS UNDER STRESS**
> **MORE STABLE AND POSITIVE MOOD**
> **INCREASED CONFIDENCE**

One of the most important benefits of good physical conditioning for athletes is greater endurance. It requires top fitness to complete in an entire game, race or competition while maintaining maximum skill.

Greater strength comes from physical training, as well. There is hardly a sport that is not helped by improved strength, or at least, toning. Increased flexibility is another essential benefit. Flexibility is crucial to being able to "stretch" to make the extra effort, reach for the fly ball, or generate torque in a golf swing. Flexibility is crucial to your athlete's overall level of performance. That is why athletes warm-up and "stretch-out" before a competition.

Being in top condition also reduces sensitivity to pain. More efficient bodily function, coupled with experience in pushing oneself, leads to more effective persistence, despite fatigue or discomfort. Good physical condition also lessens the physical effects of stress in your athlete's body; it helps to dampen the negative performance effects of stress chemicals that are released in tough situations. All of these factors come together to decrease the likelihood of injury when your athlete is in top physical shape.

The five S's of sports training are:
Stamina, speed, strength, skill and spirit:
But the greatest of these is spirit.

- **Ken Doherty,** Olympian
Track Coach Princeton, PA, Mich.
Former Meet Director, Penn Relays

One of the new things that psychology and sport psychology research is discovering is that being in good physical condition can help your athlete be tougher mentally, as well. Exercise and good physical condition can help your athlete to concentrate better and focus more on the contest. Athletes, and people who exercise regularly, have more positive attitudes about themselves and their lives. Being in good condition can help keep your athlete psyched. Athletes and others who are in good physical condition can also deal better psychologically and emotionally with stress.

Nutrition is also very important for being in top physical shape, and performing at maximum levels. So much is written about sports nutrition that it is impossible to discuss it here. If you are interested you can find much information about nutrition and sports performance.

We encourage you to read more about this, but make sure that what you read, and especially what you follow, is valid and comes from someone who knows what they are talking about. It is best to ask a sports nutritionist, with a degree and training, about the best material to read and follow.

In general though, we believe that the basics to good sports nutrition involve two simple principles. First, have your athlete make use of good healthy balanced meals on a regular basis. Secondly, limit the intake of "junk food." Help your athlete stay away from too much food that is high in cholesterol or saturated fat (chips, hot dogs, etc.) or sugar (doughnuts, candy, etc.).

STASH THE TRASH: DEFENDING AGAINST THE PSYCH-OUT

This book is about the sport psychological skills of mental toughness for athletes to perform their best or what sometimes is called "Getting Psyched Up." Just as important, however, is for your athlete to learn not to get "PSYCHED-OUT." Every competition is really a psychological contest, as well as, a physical one. The athletes with the best concentration and focus, attitude, desire, and belief in their ability are usually the winners.

Some athletes try to play "mind games" with their opponents. They try to do things to distract them, or to get them off their game or race. They try to "psych out" their rivals. There are many different psych-out techniques. They are as varied as team colors, names, and logos.

> **If you can't hit, you can't run, and can't throw,**
> **Then you've got to holler at them.**
>
> **-Solly Hemus**
> St. Louis Cardinals Player and Coach

One approach is Intimidation. This is when an opponent tries to scare your athlete by looking or talking mean. Intimidation may be more direct, such as an opponent telling your athlete how hard they will hit her, how fast they will drive by her, or how much faster they are than her.

There are techniques to "yank your chain" or "get under your skin." This is when an opponent tries to insult your athlete, in order to create anger or frustration to be distracting. An opponent might make insults about your athlete's size, speed, the way she looks, teammates, family, or boyfriend. Remember when Zidane Zidane lost his cool and probably the world cup by head butting his opponent after the player reportedly insulted his sister? This may be an honorable thing to do in life, but it is rather amateurish and foolish when an athlete gets suckered by trash talk during a game, and especially when a championship is on the line.

There is also what has been called the "Poor Me Hustle." This is when an opponent pretends that she is "just not up" for a game today or "just not into it" right now. This is the opposite of intimidation. They might say they are not feeling well, or they are tired, or they are worried about something else. Pretending to be slightly injured is a variation of this. All of these things are designed to get your athlete thinking about the opponent, to feel sorry for him or her, or to feel over-confident. Meanwhile, your athlete is really being set-up by the psych-out.

Other athletes may use fits of anger, complaints about almost everything to officials, temper tantrums, or any other behavior as a psych-out. No matter what the strategy, the purpose of the psych-out is to throw your athlete off focus, distract, or have your athlete's head be anywhere other than on the competition.

Superior athletes are not affected by psych-outs, however. There are several reasons why falling for a psych-out is the mark of a "second-class" athlete.

1) Responding to psych-out behavior *in any way*, means that the opponent has "got you." He or she now "owns" your athlete, or at least your athlete's attention. Your athlete has fallen for the "psych-trap," the oldest trick in competition.

2) Responding to the psych-out means that your athlete's focus has been lost. Concentration is being scattered and diluted. Attention is not on the game and preparation. Attention is now being centered on the "show." Your athlete is paying attention to fluff and not substance.

3) Not responding to the psych-out has a great counter-attack effect because not responding frustrates the psych-out artist. Seeing their "target" stay focused is what psych-out artists hate the most. They want to get your athlete rattled. By not responding to them and staying with personal preparation, your athlete intimidates the psych-out artist. She gets them wondering why their psych-out attempt is not working. They will begin to think about trying even harder to psych out your athlete which gets them away from their own competition preparation. By not responding, your athlete makes the opponent worry, and shows them just how mentally tough she is.

4) Especially in team sports, it is impossible to contribute total performance if concentration is distracted. And if the psych-out is designed to create anger, your athlete might just respond in a way that hampers performance, affects team performance, and even draws penalties.

5) Winning athletes usually don't have time for psych-out games. They are too busy preparing themselves physically and psychologically for their own performance. They know their energy is better spent preparing themselves, rather than trying to affect their opponent.

There are several specific strategies an athlete can use to defend against the Psych-Out.

DEFENDING AGAINST THE PSYCH-OUT

1) Have your athlete practice and develop the discipline to stay focused on their personal preparation and competition. The self-regulation and the concentration training techniques we talk about later in this manual will help your athlete do this. Also, help your athlete develop a specific pre-competition preparation routine that is a good "warm-up," both physically and psychologically.

2) If your athlete starts to be distracted by psych-out behavior, she can "talk to herself." The chapter on "Self-Talk" later in this manual will help you with this. Help your athlete develop ways to talk herself through the psych-out. Help your athlete to remind herself what is going on, and not to fall for any psych-out tricks. Help your athlete to self-talk in ways that are relaxing, help her to focus, and return concentration to the competition.

3) Help you athlete to learn to walk away. Give her a strategy to pay attention to something else. Coach the lesson that it is crucial to ignore the acting and the trash from the psych-out artist.

4) Athletes can also defend the psych-out by hanging out with a teammate, or teammates, who can help them to regain their focus and concentration. It can be very effective for an athlete to work with another teammate to develop ways to avoid being drawn by psych-outs.

5) Help your young athlete focus on her own pre-competition preparation. Remember that psych-out artists want a response from your athlete, and hate it when they are ignored. Staying focused turns the tables on them. Their psych-out attempt can easily boomerang and affect them more than your athlete.

A well-focused, confident and prepared athlete is very intimidating to opponents. That is all the "psych-out" your athlete needs.

A WINNER'S APPROACH TO LOSING

Winning is easy. Not necessarily the process of winning, which requires hard work, dedication, training, hours of practice, desire, belief, and talent; but enjoying and dealing with winning is easy. It feels good and is to be enjoyed. Losing is much different, however.

Losing tests an athlete's character. It is hard to feel the pain of losing. It can seem hard to go on after a loss, but mentally tough athletes do. Losing is a part of all sports and even part of the experience of winners.

> **If you can't accept losing, you can't win**
>
> **- Vince Lombardi**
> Coach, Giants, Packers & Redskins
> 2-time Super Bowl Champion
> NFL Hall of Fame

Even the greatest athletes have lost, and do lose. The key is in the winner's approach to losing. Being a smart athlete means learning how to use a loss as a tool to become a better athlete. You can help your young athlete come to understand this. A winner's approach to losing consists of doing the following:

HELP YOUR ATHLETE ACCEPT THE LOSS

Losing is painful, but winning athletes learn to cope with the pain. They are able to do this by putting the contest and the loss in perspective. Help your young athlete understand that the thrill of sport means that someone will win......and someone will lose. Winners let the loss go, and move on to prepare for the next competition. Winning athletes, even if they lose, epitomize the words of famous Chicago Bears former player and Coach Mike Ditka who said:

You never really lose until you stop trying.

HELP YOUR ATHLETE LEARN FROM THE LOSS

Part of developing, getting better, and becoming highly skilled is learning from mistakes. Mistakes are great teachers, especially if they are used to get smarter and are not repeated. Success is the result of fixing mistakes. One of the greatest coaches of all time, Vince Lombardi said:

It's not whether you get knocked down,
It's whether you get back up.

If your athlete loses, help him or her figure out what went wrong, work on it, improve on it, and "get back up."

HELP YOUR ATHLETE ACCEPT RESPONSIBILITY

Learning from a loss, and dealing with it like a winner, requires that your athlete accept responsibility for the changes that need to be made. Denying that improvement is needed, or trying to avoid the hard work that is necessary to step up from a loss, won't work. Blaming others, like judges, refs, coaches, teammates, the crowd, or field conditions, for the loss is an easy way out, but it gets in the way of accepting responsibility, which is necessary in order to get better. It keeps an athlete from changing and dooms him or her to repeat the same mistakes and incur future losses.

HELP YOUR ATHLETE LEARN TO SEPARATE LOSS FROM FAILURE

Remember that losing is part of any sport. Your athlete doesn't have to like it, and shouldn't like it. Almost every great athlete hates to lose. Tennis icon Jimmy Connors has said:

I hate to lose more than I like to win.

However, almost every great athlete also knows that losing is not the same as failure. They know that a loss doesn't make them or their team a failure. Basketball great Charles Barkley recognized this:

I know that I am never as good or as bad as any single performance.
I've never believed my critics or my worshipers.
And I've always been able to leave the game at the arena.

Losing doesn't change your athlete's talent or potential, and need not change their motivation to develop even further. They should accept the pain of losing, take that negative emotion, and turn it into a positive drive to excel. Another great tennis champion Jim Courier said:

It is very dangerous to have your self-worth
riding on your results as an athlete.

Winners and losers become failures when they fall victim to the negative reactions that a loss can have on confidence, motivation, or self-esteem. Sport needs to be kept in perspective, as one part of your athlete's life, and a drive for achievement. It is important and it should echo enthusiasm and joy, but it is only one aspect of life. Athletes become failures when they fail to separate losing from failing, and who they are as individuals. Help your athlete understand this, and keep a healthy and motivated perspective.

Losing is no disgrace if you've given your best.

- Jim Palmer
Baltimore Orioles Hall of Fame Pitcher
3-time World Series Champion
3-time AL Cy Young Award Winner

HELP YOUR ATHLETE TAKE PRIDE IN EFFORT AND NOT JUST OUTCOME

The idea of "**best effort**" is an important one in all sports (and all aspects of life). If your athlete performed as best she could, regardless of outcome, you should help her take pride in the effort. Your athlete can't do more than her best effort on a given day, and the mark of a great athlete is to give his or her best effort each time, and to be consistent in the quality of their effort. Remember that consistency in performance is the hallmark of great athletes. Outcomes of competitions are not controllable. Someone may be faster or more accurate than your athlete on a given day; opponents' performance is not controllable. Your athlete's effort is. Help your athlete learn to work on things within her control. Help her feel proud when she does, and when she gives her best.

LOSING IS A PART OF SPORT:

LOSE LIKE A WINNER

III

ARE THEY PSYCHED? A MENTAL TRYOUT

You are really never playing an opponent.
You are playing yourself...

      -Arthur Ashe
      Tennis Great
      Winner US Open, Australian Open, Wimbledon
      International Tennis Hall of Fame
      Namesake, Arthur Ashe Stadium, USTA Tennis Center

An important place to start, when learning psychology and mental toughness skills in sport, is to help your athlete evaluate his strengths and weaknesses in this area. As a competitor, your athlete probably has begun to develop some sport psychology skills already. The following questionnaire will help you and your athlete think about these sport psychology and mental toughness skills, and begin to introduce some more types of psychological skills that are important in sport. Based on the work of sport performance expert Dr. James Loehr, it will help your athlete assess which skills they have already developed, and which skills might need more attention and work.

By completing this self-test in an honest manner (trying to look "good" won't help) your athlete can develop his own **PSYCHOLOGICAL READINESS FOR EXCELLENCE PROFILE or PREP.**

On the next page you will find some statements about sport competition. Have your athlete read each statement and indicate how true it is for him by circling the appropriate letters. The letters mean the following:

    The letters **AT** mean the statement is   **ALWAYS TRUE** for your athlete
    The letters **OT** mean the statement is   **OFTEN TRUE** for your athlete
    The letters **ST** mean the statement is   **SOMETIMES TRUE** for your athlete
    The letters **RT** mean the statement is   **RARELY TRUE** for your athlete
    The letters **NT** mean the statement is   **NEVER TRUE** for your athlete

For example, if the first statement is SOMETIMES TRUE for your athlete,
the statement would look like this:

```
┌─────────────────────────────────────────────────────────────┐
│                                                               │
│      1.  I have a routine I do before each competition to prepare │
│    mentally                                                   │
│                                                               │
│                    AT    OT   (ST)   RT    NT                 │
│                    5     4     3 )   2     1                  │
│                                                               │
└─────────────────────────────────────────────────────────────┘
```

If the second statement is ALWAYS TRUE for your athlete, it would look like this:

```
┌─────────────────────────────────────────────────────────────┐
│                                                               │
│      2.  The tougher the competition, the better I like it    │
│                                                               │
│                  (AT)   OT   ST   RT    NT                    │
│                   5 )   4    3    2     1                     │
│                                                               │
└─────────────────────────────────────────────────────────────┘
```

Now go ahead and have your athlete circle the best choice for all the statements.

1.   I have a routine I do before each competition to prepare my focus.

                                        AT   OT   ST   RT   NT
                                        5   4   3   2   1

2.   The tougher the competition, the better I like it.

                                        AT   OT   ST   RT   NT
                                        5   4   3   2   1

3.   If I'm nervous before a competition, I can calm myself down.

                                        AT   OT   ST   RT   NT
                                        5   4   3   2   1

4.   When competing, I can easily lose my concentration.

                                        AT   OT   ST   RT   NT
                                        1   2   3   4   5

5.   Before a competition, I am able to imagine myself performing well.

                                        AT   OT   ST   RT   NT
                                        5   4   3   2   1

21

6.   I think about positive things when competing.

	AT	OT	ST	RT	NT
	5	4	3	2	1

7.   I plan good meals so I can perform my best.

	AT	OT	ST	RT	NT
	5	4	3	2	1

8.   I can forget about everything except competing before a contest.

	AT	OT	ST	RT	NT
	5	4	3	2	1

9.   If something goes wrong, I get easily "shook up."

	AT	OT	ST	RT	NT
	1	2	3	4	5

10.   I can adjust from a mistake and return to competing confidently.

	AT	OT	ST	RT	NT
	5	4	3	2	1

11.   I get angry and upset easily.

	AT	OT	ST	RT	NT
	1	2	3	4	5

12.   I mentally practice my sport skills just like I physically practice them.

	AT	OT	ST	RT	NT
	5	4	3	2	1

13.   I often think discouraging things about my performance.

	AT	OT	ST	RT	NT
	1	2	3	4	5

14.   I try to get at least seven hours of sleep each night.

	AT	OT	ST	RT	NT
	5	4	3	2	1

15. I can get myself into a special focused state before my competition starts.

	AT	OT	ST	RT	NT
	5	4	3	2	1

16. I worry I will "choke" or "freeze" at a critical time in a competition.

	AT	OT	ST	RT	NT
	1	2	3	4	5

17. I wish my body wouldn't get so nervous before I compete.

	AT	OT	ST	RT	NT
	1	2	3	4	5

18. My mind stays focused only on performing well when I am competing.

	AT	OT	ST	RT	NT
	5	4	3	2	1

19. If I imagine myself performing, I can see _and feel_ my performance, too.

	AT	OT	ST	RT	NT
	5	4	3	2	1

20. I worry about making a mistake even before I start to compete.

	AT	OT	ST	RT	NT
	1	2	3	4	5

21. I try to avoid "junk food" (candy, doughnuts, chips, etc.).

	AT	OT	ST	RT	NT
	5	4	3	2	1

22. I have a special confident feeling I can create for myself to do well.

	AT	OT	ST	RT	NT
	5	4	3	2	1

23. I believe in myself and my ability.

	AT	OT	ST	RT	NT
	5	4	3	2	1

24.   **I wish I could be calmer before I compete.**

                                        AT   OT   ST   RT   NT
                                         1   2   3   4   5

25.   **My mind wanders while I am competing.**

                                        AT   OT   ST   RT   NT
                                         1   2   3   4   5

26.   **Imagining myself perform is easy for me.**

                                        AT   OT   ST   RT   NT
                                         5   4   3   2   1

27.   **I often criticize myself and get down on my performance.**

                                        AT   OT   ST   RT   NT
                                         1   2   3   4   5

28. I engage in a regular physical conditioning program.

                                        AT   OT   ST   RT   NT
                                         5   4   3   2   1

PSYCHOLOGICAL READINESS FOR EXCELLENCE PROFILE (PREP) SCORE SHEET

PSYCHING UP	CONFIDENCE	POSITIVE PSYCH	FOCUS	IMAGERY USE	SELF-TALK	PHYSICAL CONDITIONING
1.	2.	3.	4.	5.	6.	7.
8.	9.	10.	11.	12.	13.	14.
15.	16.	17.	18.	19.	20.	21.
22.	23.	24.	25.	26.	27.	28.
TOTALS						

PSYCHOLOGICAL READINESS FOR EXCELLENCE PROFILE (PREP)

PSYCHING UP	CONFIDENCE	POSITIVE PSYCH	FOCUS	IMAGERY USE	SELF-TALK	PHYSICAL CONDITIONING

```
20
19              ELITE PERFORMER
18---------------------------------------------------------------------
17
16              YOU'RE A STARTER
15---------------------------------------------------------------------
14
13
12
11
10              YOU MADE THE TEAM
09
08
07
06
05---------------------------------------------------------------------
04              STILL TRYING OUT
03
02
01
00
```

PSYCHING UP	CONFIDENCE	POSITIVE PSYCH	FOCUS	IMAGERY USE	SELF-TALK	PHYSICAL CONDITIONING

After you have completed the self-test, return to the tally sheet on the previous page, take the number your athlete circled for each question and put it in the appropriate place on the score sheet. After you have transferred all the scores, add up the total for each column (Psyching Up, Confidence, etc.), and write the total in space marked TOTALS.

Finally, take the total score for each skill and plot it on the graph of your athlete's PREP. This will give you a picture of your athlete's Sport Psychology Skills; which ones are strong and which ones need work. The higher the score for each skill, the stronger it is. High scores suggest good psychological skills, or factors that enhance performance as part of mental toughness.

What does your athlete's PREP mean? You and your athlete will have a much better understanding of this after you have read this manual and are more familiar with the psychological aspects of performance. However, a brief description as an introduction is as follows:

Psyching Up refers to the general ability of your athlete to get into the best mindset to compete and perform at the optimal level. This may be a matter of "pumping up," or it may be a matter of calming down. *Confidence* describes the degree of your athlete's belief in his ability to perform in competition. *Positive Psych* is a measure of the ability to be positive and at maximum readiness for competition. *Focus* reflects the ability to maintain concentration and attention during competition. *Imagery Use* refers to the ability to mentally rehearse skills or plays and prepare for specific competitions or aspects of a game. *Self-Talk* is related to a specific psychological performance technique that affects how thinking during practice and competition influences performance. Finally, since the mind and body are connected, the last category is a measure of behaviors that promote optimal *Physical Condition*.

On the graph, the higher the score, the stronger your athlete's psychological skill is in that area. A score of 0 to 5 means that it is still "TRY-OUT TIME:" your athlete's psychological skills and mental toughness can use a lot of work. A score of 6 to 15 means that your athlete is at the psychological equivalent of having "MADE THE TEAM:" your athlete is developing some skills and is ready to refine them through practice and competition.

A score of 16 to 18 means your athlete's sport psychology skills and mental toughness are that of a "STARTER:" the skills are translating into a higher level performance. A score of 19 or 20 means that your athlete's sport psychology and mental toughness skills are those of an "ELITE PERFORMER."

Remember that the score depends on how honest your athlete was in answering the questions. If there are some low scores, don't be discouraged. Use them as a motivation to develop these skills. If your athlete has some high scores, see if they can be strengthened even further, to become an even more "mentally tough" athlete.

IV
SCORING POINTS AND GOALS:
GOAL SETTING

Failure to prepare, is preparing to fail.

-John Wooden
Ten-time National Champion Basketball Coach

Winning races, scoring points, and reaching for dreams require **setting goals** for practice and performance. Why is goal setting so important? Goals are the path that leads your athlete to superior performance. They are the roadmap that tells your athlete where he or she is going. Without such direction, you and your athlete wouldn't know where to go, if you're getting there, or even if you've made it.

Goals **IMPROVE PERFORMANCE**. Goals also **IMPROVE PRACTICE**. They measure progress, and determine whether or not all the effort is being effective. Goals **IMPROVE MOTIVATION**. Seeing gains helps to keep up motivation when the training gets hard. Goals can also help to reduce some of the boredom of training by letting your athlete see how their efforts turn into real progress. Achieving goals results **in PRIDE, SATISFACTION,** and **SELF-CONFIDENCE**.

These results of goal setting are summarized below.

RESULTS OF GOAL SETTING

➢ IMPROVED PERFORMANCE
➢ IMPROVED PRACTICE
➢ IMPROVED MOTIVATION
➢ IMPROVED PRIDE, SATISFACTION & CONFIDENCE

Goal setting is one of the most basic tools for developing winning performance in sport, but it is also one that is too often overlooked or ignored. Without goal setting, successful performance is a matter of luck, rather than planning. Without goal setting, only the luckiest and most talented athletes will achieve their potential. With goal setting, any athlete can reach the peak of his or her ability.

But, how do you make goal setting effective? Just as with physical practice, your athlete's efforts should be efficient and productive.

There are several strategies to maximizing goal-setting, and they are summarized below:

<u>WAYS TO MAKE GOAL SETTING WORK FOR YOUR ATHLETE</u>

- **GOALS SHOULD BE SHORT-TERM**
- **GOALS SHOULD BE LONG-TERM**
- **GOALS SHOULD BE STATED POSITIVELY**
- **GOALS SHOULD FOCUS ON TECHNIQUE**
- **GOALS SHOULD BE MEASURABLE**
- **GOALS SHOULD BE REALISTIC BUT DIFFICULT**
- **GOALS SHOULD BE SET BY YOUR ATHLETE**
- **GOALS SHOULD BE REVIEWED BY YOUR COACH**
- **GOALS SHOULD HAVE TIME LINES**
- **GOALS SHOULD BE RATED BY IMPORTANCE**
- **GOALS SHOULD BE OF DIFFERENT TYPES**
- **GOALS SHOULD BE SET FOR THE TEAM & INDIVIDUALS**
- **GOALS SHOULD BE WRITTEN DOWN**
- **GOALS SHOULD BE FLEXIBLE**

You always have to focus in life on what you want to achieve.

-Michael Jordan
6-time NBA Champion
5-time NBA MVP
10-time NBA Scoring Champion
Hall of Fame

We all like to think about doing well in the future, maybe setting records, winning championships, or achieving our dreams. However, the path to a successful future is through **SHORT-TERM GOALS**. Short-term goals start with daily practice goals, or knowing what your athlete wants to accomplish in each practice. There are also weekly goals, what your athlete wants to achieve on a week-to-week basis. And, finally, there are monthly goals, which are still short-term goals, but involve slightly greater improvement over a longer period of time.

While the short-term goals lead us to future performance and achievements, your athlete also needs **LONG-TERM GOALS** to help her see what she is working towards. Long-term goals are goals that span several months, over a year, and an Ultimate Sports Achievement goal (USA). The USA may be earning the position of team captain, a state championship, an athletic scholarship, succeeding at a Division I school, or an Olympic try-out. There is nothing wrong with dreaming big and desiring such success, but goals must be used to help your athlete go as far as possible towards that dream.

When goals are being set, **GOALS SHOULD BE STATED POSITIVELY**. This means that your athlete should decide what *to do or achieve, rather than what not to do.* Sometimes athletes set goals in terms of things they want to avoid, such as "not have my mind wander during the game." A better way to state this goal would be "To strengthen my concentration by practicing my concentration skills more often" or "To stay focused on my race strategy more of the time." Stating goals in the negative, leads to your athlete thinking about the very things she doesn't want to think about.

The kinds of goals that are most effective in helping athletes achieve their dreams are **SKILL-FOCUSED GOALS**. It is ok, and very motivating, to think about "setting a record" or "running a 4.4," but setting this kind of goal doesn't guide your athlete on HOW to set the record or make that time. Achievements are the result of developing *skills* that lead to a win or record time, so a better goal might be "to create more drive off my back leg."

To make goal setting effective, whenever possible, the goals that are set must be **MEASURABLE GOALS**. This means you and your athlete must decide how you will measure the progress that is being made. So, rather than set a goal like "to be faster in my turns," you might try (1) "To practice 25 perfect push-offs per practice" and/or (2) "To increase the distance on my push-off by 2.0 feet."

The will to win is grossly overrated.
The will to prepare is far more important.

-Bobby Knight, Basketball Coach
3-time National Champion
Hall of Fame

It is necessary to set **REALISTIC, BUT DIFFICULT GOALS**. A simple definition of a difficult goal is any goal that is greater than your athlete's present performance. Doing better always takes effort. Improvement comes in small steps, so any increase or improvement in performance is good progress. Becoming impatient, and setting goals that are too far above your athlete's current level, will not help them get there faster. In fact, if goals are too extreme, your athlete is likely to fail, become discouraged, and unmotivated. Setting goals that provide a steady rate of successful improvement will get your athlete to her USA with maximum efficiency.

Goal setting should involve **GOALS THAT ARE SET BY YOUR ATHLETE**. She will know best what is important to her, what she wants to achieve, and *how hard she is willing to work to achieve it.* When goals are set by your athlete, they are more meaningful and more motivating.

When setting goals, your athlete should have her **GOALS REVIEWED BY THE COACH**. This is especially true for short-term and longer term goals. The dream goal or USA goal is a little different, however. This is something that is very special and personal to your athlete, as it is for each and every athlete. This is something your athlete should share with you, her coach, or anyone else only if she wants to do so.

For other goals, however, while your athlete should design her own goals, the coach has the expertise to know if these are the goals and priorities that your athlete needs to work on. It makes no sense to waste time working on something that will not help your athlete's performance. The coach can provide guidance in refining the goals effectively, assure that the proposed goals are reasonable and measurable, and can give feedback on your athlete's progress. The coach can also help if things seem stuck. Have your athlete set goals, but have them reviewed, and be open to comments about them.

Your athlete's goals should have **TIME LINES**. There should be some estimate on how long it will take to achieve a goal. This might be influenced by the type or difficulty of the goal, or, it may be influenced by how long your athlete has to get ready for the season or upcoming competition. Having a time line also helps monitor progress so that you know if there needs to be a change in some aspect of training. Thinking about short-term and long-term goals helps to set time lines.

It is also important to **RATE GOALS BY IMPORTANCE**. This means that your athlete should rate which goals are the most important, and which ones need to be achieved first. This will prevent wasted time and effort. In every sport, there are many skills and goals to be improved or reached. With so many goals to pursue, it is very easy to become confused or misdirected. Therefore, deciding which goals are most crucial will show which goals are most deserving of hard work and effort. This is where the coach's input can be especially helpful.

Your athlete should consider having **DIFFERENT TYPES OF GOALS**. While the main focus of sport training is to improve skills, be part of the competition, and perform as best as possible, there are other types of goals that your athlete might set. A very important goal is to have fun, because it is key to keeping the sports experience in perspective. While working hard is essential to athletic success, so is having fun. NO athlete can maintain motivation if he or she is not enjoying what they are doing. Other types of goals may be to meet other athletes, make friends, travel to other cities, learn about different styles of competition, or develop lifetime exercise habits.

TEAM GOALS can be essential for improvement, as well. All of the suggestions already made about setting effective goals for your athlete's personal performance apply to setting team goals too. It is important that as a team, the athletes and coach sit down and decide on what goals they want to achieve.

Your athlete will be more successful if she can **PUT THE GOALS IN WRITING.** When your athlete writes down goals, it is harder to forget about them. By writing them, your athlete already had to think about them one more time. When they are in front of your athlete in written form, they jump out and grab him or her. It is useful to hang them where they will be seen frequently, as reminders of commitment. Additionally, when goals are written, they are easier to analyze and review, in order to see if they meet the guidelines suggested above, such as being stated positively, being measurable, or being realistic.

Finally, **GOALS SHOULD BE FLEXIBLE.** While you want your athlete to stick to the projected goals, you also want her to learn that there are times when adjustments need to be made. Help your athlete to learn how to make those adjustments. There may be changes in the season or competition schedule, practice times, field conditions, or even an injury which means that your athlete can not pursue goals in the way they were originally planned. Part of successful goal setting is to be able to adjust goals when necessary. Flexibility should be a goal as well.

On the next page you will find some practice drills to help your athlete learn to set goals. Have your athlete fill in expectations for the different types of goals listed. Then go over them together, and with the coach, to make sure they meet the rules for effective goal setting, and are what needs to worked on. Have the coach place his or her initials on the coach's "OK" line when approved.

GOAL SETTING FOR SPORT ACHIEVEMENTS

MY ULTIMATE SPORT ACHIEVEMENT (USA) GOAL IS:

_____

_____

MY DAILY PRACTICE GOALS FOR TODAY ARE:

_____

_____

THE WAY I MEASURE THESE GOALS ARE:

_____

_____

MY PRACTICE GOALS FOR THIS WEEK ARE:

_____

_____

THE WAY I MEASURE THESE GOALS ARE:

_____

_____

COACH'S OK_____

WHAT I WANT TO ACCOMPLISH THIS MONTH IS:

_____

_____

THE WAY I WILL MEASURE THIS IS:

_____

_____

MY PERFORMANCE GOAL FOR THIS YEAR IS:

_____

_____

THE WAY I WILL MEASURE THIS IS:

_____

_____

OTHER SPORT GOALS FOR ME ARE:

_____

_____

THE WAY I WILL MEASURE THIS:

_____

_____

HOW LONG THIS WILL TAKE ME TO ACCOMLISH:

_____

COACH'S OK _____

V

THE STARTING WHISTLE:
PSYCHING UP

If the mind can conceive it
And your heart can believe it,
You can achieve it

-Cal Botterill
Canadian Sport Psychologist

Getting "Psyched" or "Psyching Up" is something that most athletes and coaches talk about. What do they really mean? Psyching Up can mean different things to different athletes. We believe that psyching up refers to an athlete preparing mentally to perform at a maximum level.

This book contains many suggestions and techniques that allow athletes to maximize their performance. It is important that your athlete take the techniques that work best for him and put them together in a pre-game or pre-competition routine. We call this the **Mental Warm-up**.

It will be helpful for your athlete to choose ways to prepare mentally before each contest. He will also want to prepare psychologically before each practice, for this will result in maximum effort and results from each practice session. As important, is mental preparation before practices which will provide the opportunity to master sport psychology mental toughness techniques to use during competitions. Psyching will transfer to the actual competitions.

While being psyched and having enthusiasm doesn't replace hard work and talent, it makes everything go more smoothly. There are several ways that athletes can psych themselves up. Can you and your athlete name some, and place them in the space below?

WAYS THAT ATHLETES WARM-UP MENTALLY

_____

_____

_____

_____

How did you do? Did you include ways that your athlete warms-up mentally? Here are some typical ways athletes psychologically warm-up.

WAYS THAT ATHLETES WARM-UP MENTALLY

> PHYSICAL WARM-UPS

> MUSIC

> LIKE-PSYCHS

> CUE WORDS

> CUE IMAGES

> SELF-CONFIDENCE STATEMENTS

Physical Warm-ups are usually part of the pre-competition preparation that every athletic team goes through. They are not only a good way to prepare physically for the competition, but they also prepare your athlete psychologically, as well. Remember the mind and body are connected. They function as one, and each affects the other. When your athlete does physical warm-ups and begins to feel ready physically, this sets the stage for feeling good psychologically and mentally tough, as well.

Music is probably the most popular way that athletes prepare mentally for competition. It should come as no surprise that music can have a huge affect on the way your athlete feels. Quiet, peaceful music can make your athlete feel calm and laid-back. Hard rock, Hip-Hop, or even a powerful symphony can get your athlete pumped and "ready to move."

Therefore, making a pre-competition music mix that your athlete favors can help your athlete psych-up. It will help your athlete develop the right mindset for competition, whether that is really pumped-up or a controlled, relaxed focus. Selecting a specific song or constructing a special mix is much more effective than simply listening to the radio. If this mix is also used to maximize readiness for practices, it will transfer to the competition, as well. However, some athletes prefer to have a separate mix for practice versus competition.

Many athletes use **Cue Words** to prepare psychologically and call-up the mental toughness mindset. Cue words are single words, or short phrases, that convey a powerful, positive emotional message. They are used to provide positive emotion and to focus your athlete on important aspects of the game.

Examples might be the words "Power," Strong," "Speed," "Explode," or the phrases "Do it, "Nail it, "Drive it." Other examples of more specifically focused words and phrases might be "Focus," "Control," or "Extend," "Reach," "Grip," "Teamwork," "Streamline," or "Fast."

Some athletes use **Cue Images** to help psych up. There are two types of imagery that can be used. The first type, similar to cue words are pictures and images that come to the athlete's mind and represent power, speed, form, strength or whatever characteristic is needed.

34

> **I visualize the blood surging through my muscles**
> **with every repetition and every set I do.**
>
> **-Rachel McLish**
> Champion Body-builder
> 2-time Ms.Olympia

For example, some athletes try to image electricity popping and flowing through their muscles as they get "all charged up." Some athletes see images of a tiger, cheetah or leopard speeding across a field, their muscles rippling with power. They feel the power and rhythm, and super-impose this on their own muscles. Some athletes see their leg muscles working like the powerful wheels of a steam train engine. Other athletes image a cool, blue fog spreading over them to relax them and narrow their focus to the game. Whatever image produces the level of emotional intensity your athlete needs is one that can be very effective in maximizing performance.

The other type of imagery is performance enhancing imagery of a particular skill, play, or aspect of the competition. This is mental rehearsal of your athlete's performance, and the keys to making performance-enhancing imagery effective are discussed in Chapter 8.

Like-Psychs refers to spending time or "hanging out" right before the competition with teammates who demonstrate the amount of "psych" that your athlete needs. If your athlete needs to get really psyched up, suggest hanging out with the teammates who are the loudest, most demonstrative, and energetic. If your athlete needs only a little psych, or needs to relax before the contest, suggest hanging out with the teammates who are more laid-back. Your athlete can promote mental readiness by staying around the teammates who have the level of pump that he needs.

Self-Confidence Statements are another way to psych up by having your athlete say positive things to him or herself. Examples might be:

> ➤ **I'm Ready**

> ➤ **I'm Feeling Good**

> ➤ **I'm Feeling Sharp**

> ➤ **I'm Feeling On**

> ➤ **We're Well-Coached**

The chapter on championship thinking and self-talk will provide some additional suggestions how to make self-confidence statements work the best for your athlete.

Finally, in case you were wondering whether or not psyching really makes a difference, the answer is YES. Among other research and evidence, this was nicely shown in a sport psychology experiment done by famous sport psychologist Dr. Mike Mahoney and his colleague way back in 1978. This was a study on the effects of psyching-up on grip, or hand strength, in weightlifters (Shelton & Mahoney, 1978).

At a national weight lifting championship, weightlifters were divided into two groups, a psyching group and a non-psyching group. Grip strength was measured by a hand dynamometer. There were three trials for each group. The results are summarized below.

In the first trial, individuals in both groups were told to immediately grip the dynamometer as hard as possible on the "go" signal. In the second trial, individuals were told to count backwards from 100, subtracting seven each time until they heard the "go" signal (always thirty seconds later), and then grip the dynamometer as hard as possible. The counting was done to distract the weightlifters, and to prevent them from psyching-up on their own before gripping.

The difference was in the third trial. This time, the psyching group was told to psych-up until they heard the "go" signal (thirty seconds later), and then grip the dynamometer as strongly as possible. The non-psyching group was again made to count backwards from one-hundred until they heard the "go" signal (also thirty seconds later), and then grip as strongly as possible. Thus, the point was to compare strength in the third trial where the one group was able to psych-up, while the other group could not psych-up. The results are in the table below:

PSYCHING AND GRIP STRENGTH IN COMPETITVE WEIGHTLIFTERS			
TRIALS	1	2	3
Psyching Group	52.13 kg.	51.46 kg.	54.93 kg
Non-Psyching Group	50.85 kg.	50.65 kg.	49.12 kg

As can be seen from the results, the psyching group demonstrated greater handgrip strength (54.9 kilograms) than the non-psyching group (49.12 kilograms). It is also noteworthy that the psyching group showed the greatest strength on their third trial, which was the only trial during which they psyched-up. The results also show that it is unlikely that "practice" was a factor, because the non-psyching group demonstrated decreasing strength across the trials.

ESP: PSYCHING UP INTO THE ENHANCED PERFORMANCE STATE

We just discussed ways for your athlete to get "psyched up" and mentally prepared for a competition. Many times, just the excitement of the competition will help to get your athlete "pumped" and ready to compete. However, this excitement can be unpredictable, and it may not get your athlete pumped enough **OR**, very often the excitement of an upcoming race can get your athlete **too** pumped up. In fact, being too pumped is usually the problem for athletes, especially in important games, or at critical moments in the competition.

In formal terms, the degree of "pump" is called your athlete's *level of physical arousal.* It is also known as the level of activation. Physical arousal, or activation, is the result of the chemical adrenaline, along with other stress related chemicals, that our bodies produce when we are faced with a challenge. The outpouring of adrenaline can be a powerful performance enhancing response to a challenge. This will occur when the adrenaline "dump" is *trained and restrained.* When it is untrained and unrestrained, when it is too much or out of control, it can degrade performance.

Sport psychology research, and our experience, shows that athletes perform best when they have the "right amount" of physical arousal. The level of physical arousal is related to the quality of your athlete's performance in a relationship as shown below.

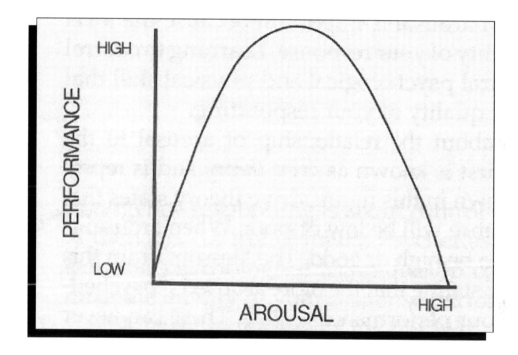

This is often called the Upside-Down-U (or Inverted-U) model of physical arousal and performance. It is actually called the Yerkes-Dodson Law, and comes from military research conducted at the beginning of the last century.

What this diagram means is that when your athlete's level of physical arousal is too low, or your athlete isn't pumped enough, performance will be less than optimal. This is where your athlete will benefit from the techniques we discussed to increase arousal.

However, the model also says that too much arousal, or getting too psyched, also interferes with performance. If your athlete is too pumped, both physical and mental skills like coordination and concentration can falter. There are techniques to moderate arousal, as well.

Therefore, your athlete should try to get himself to the best level of physical arousal. This is called by various names, including the OPTIMAL AROUSAL LEVEL (OAL), IDEAL PERFORMANCE STATE (IPS), or OPTIMAL ENERGY ZONE (OEZ). We like to call this level your athlete's **O-ZONE** or **Optimal Zone of Natural Excellence.** We call getting to the O-ZONE, developing or switching on your athlete's **ESP** or **Enhanced State for Performance.**

How much psych is right for your athlete? This is something your athlete will learn with experience. There are two techniques described by famous Canadian Sport Psychologist, Dr. Terry Orlick, which your athlete can use to define his O-ZONE and his personal ESP.

One way is to have your athlete close his eyes and think about a past game or competition in which he did very well, a game or competition where performance was almost perfect, confidence was strong, and fun was high. Then have your athlete think about how pumped up or relaxed he felt at that time. Your athlete can use the gauge below to circle how pumped or laid back he felt. Zero is really laid back and relaxed; ten is as pumped up as he ever felt in competition.

MY LEVEL OF PSYCH DURING MY PAST BEST PERFORMANCES

0   1   2   3   4   5   6   7   8   9   10
(REALLY LAID BACK)   **(REALLY PUMPED UP)**

This should give you and your athlete an idea of what level of psych is associated with playing the best. It should provide a good idea of how pumped (or relaxed) your athlete should try to be before a competition. You will know this is accurate if you find the same level of arousal when your athlete thinks of other ideal performances.

Then have your athlete recall games or competitions where things did not go well, where performance was much less than expected. Once again using the gauge below have your athlete rate how pumped or laid back she or he felt. Again, zero is really laid back and relaxed; ten is as pumped up as they ever felt in competition.

Now look for patterns. Is there a difference between the levels of arousal for your athlete between the best and worst performances? This can help your athlete discover the O-ZONE by showing what level of pump works and which level does not.

Another method to help you discover the best level of psych for your athlete is what we call **PSYCHING-EVALUATION PRACTICE (PEP)**. This involves your athlete psyching-up to different levels of pump before different practice sessions and evaluating how well practice went. For example, at one practice have your athlete try to stay really calm and mellow and then evaluate the performance and confidence during that practice. At another practice, have your athlete get as pumped as possible and then evaluate quality of performance and confidence during that practice.

Use the gauge below to judge how pumped your athlete was, and whether this was the level of pump targeted.

MY LEVEL OF PSYCH DURING PRACTICE

0   1   2   3   4   5   6   7   8   9   10
(REALLY LAID-BACK)   **(REALLY PUMPED UP)**

Use the next gauge below to rate the quality of performance at that level of pump. Zero represents disappointing or low quality performance, and ten represents great performance.

THE QUALITY OF MY PERFORMANCE DURING PRACTICE

0   1   2   3   4   5   6   7   8   9   10
(LESS THAN EXPECTED)   **(REALLY GREAT)**

Compare the ratings of your athlete's level of psych or pump with his quality of performance to see if your can discover a relationship. He will need to do this several times at different levels of psych to see if a relationship exists, and whether or not it is consistent.

Once your athlete discovers a relationship and what level is his O-ZONE, it will be useful to use the techniques in this book to get to the O-ZONE and get the ESP switched on.

A very important lesson and concept here is that the O-ZONE and Enhance State of Performance are unique for every athlete.

The great jockey Steve Cauthen offered:

I don't psych myself up. I psych myself down.
I think clearer when I'm not psyched up.

Remember not all athletes need to be really pumped before a competition, nor do all athletes need to be really relaxed. One of the biggest mistakes that coaches and parents make is believing that all athletes need to get "really pumped" for their performances. When we use the term psyching-up or getting pumped, we mean preparing psychologically, whether that is getting really energized or settling down. Help your athlete discover the best ESP for him, and then achieve it.

Research (Ferrell et al., 2006) shows that the ESP or getting into the "Zone," is a real and unique psychological and physiological state; it is a different brain state of awareness. When athletes are placed in a brain scanner (fMRI) and asked to "psych up," it is possible to see changes in their brain states.

> **When you walk on the court, clear your mind of everything**
> **unrelated to the goal of playing the match as well as you can.**
>
> **-Stan Smith**
> 2-time Grand Slam Champion
> Wimbledon & US Open Champion

Remember, once your athlete has a good idea of what level of pump works best for achieving ideal performance in a game or match, he should use self-regulation techniques, the pumping up or up-regulation techniques already discussed to increase activation, or the down-regulation techniques we will discuss next to calm down and decrease activation. This is the key to switching on or getting into his ESP (Enhanced State for Performance).

VI
TIME OUT:
STRESS AND STAYING RELAXED

You have to be able to center yourself...

- Kareem Abdul-Jabbar
6-tme NBA MVP
6-time NBA Champion
19-time NBA All-Star
Hall of Fame

Stress is often, too often, an unfortunate part of sport and competition. It is stress that leads to the excessive release of adrenaline, and other stress chemicals in the body, which can make it hard to switch on the ESP, and can reduce the quality of performance. There are many situations that athletes find stressful, but in general, competitive stress:

> **Occurs whenever your athlete cares about the outcome of the challenge and there is an imbalance between the demands if the challenge and your athlete's perception of his or her ability to meet those demands.**

This means that any time your athlete (or your athlete's team) does not feel up to meeting the challenge of the game, stress will occur. There are many reasons why athletes might not feel up to the challenge. Maybe they feel that they are not skilled enough; maybe they feel they didn't practice enough; maybe they feel the other team has faster swimsuits, faster cleats, better equipment, or a super secret nutrition diet plan! The reason doesn't matter so much as your athlete's *belief* that she is not up to the challenge. If your athlete feels up to the challenge, then there is no stress. If your athlete does not feel up to the challenge, stress will be present.

The second important part of the definition is that stress comes from your athlete's *perception* that she is not ready to face the challenge. Due to the fact that this is a personal perception, it explains why one athlete may feel stressed in a given situation and another athlete will not feel stressed in the same situation.

The key point here is that your athlete's perception and belief can be changed and controlled. That is the purpose of doing sport psychology and mental toughness training, to develop psychological skills and confidence so your athlete can manage emotion and perceptions of readiness to succeed.

Finally, stress occurs only when your athlete cares about the outcome of the competition. If your athlete doesn't really care about the results, or the quality of her performance, stress is not a factor. However, every true athlete, no matter what age, cares about the results, so stress can occur and will be a bigger problem if mental toughness skills have not been trained.

There are some typical situations that are stressful for athletes. Before they are described, it might be good for your athlete to write down any situations in her sport that she finds stressful.

SITUATIONS THAT ARE STRESSFUL FOR ME

_____

_____

_____

From our experience, some common situations that are stressful for athletes include:

- **A REALLY IMPORTANT GAME**
- **A REALLY IMPORTANT PLAY, ROUND, OR SHOT**
- **WORRYING WHAT THE COACH IS THINKING**
- **WORRYING WHAT PARENTS ARE THINKING**
- **WORRYING WHAT FRIENDS ARE THINKING**
- **LOSING**

Notice that stress comes from situations directly related to the contest, but it can also be related to personal feelings. Sport psychology and mental toughness techniques minimize, or erase, these types of concerns because they can help your athlete maintain confidence and focus on performance so quality can be maximized.

Another important aspect of controlling competitive stress is to control the reactions and symptoms of stress. What are the feelings of stress? Some of these signs are listed below:

SIGNS OF STRESS

- **"BUTTERFLIES" IN THE STOMACH**
- **SWEATY PALMS**
- **TIGHT MUSCLES**
- **DRY MOUTH**
- **FEELING TIRED**
- **FEELING RESTLESS**
- **NEEDING TO "GO TO THE BATHROOM"**
- **BLURRY VISION**
- **TOURBLE CONCENTRATING**
- **SLOW OR IMPULSIVE DECISION-MAKING**

These are common signs of stress in athletes. Your athlete may have experienced some of these, or your athlete might have some reactions to stress that are unique.

While stress affects how an athlete's body functions, it can also negatively affect *performance* for an athlete. The performance effects of stress are listed below:

PERFORMANCE EFFECTS OF STRESS

- **REDUCED AWARENESS OF THE GAME OR FIELD**
- **INCREASED FIXATION ON THE SIGNS OF STRESS**
- **DECREASED ABILITY TO TOLERATE FRUSTRATION OR PAIN**
- **INCREASED FIXATION ON MISTAKES**
- **DECREASED CONCENTRATION**
- **INCREASED MISTAKES AND INJURY**

When athletes become stressed, the have a **reduced awareness of the game, field, court, course, mat, lane or range.** They are less able to be aware of what is going on around them, where their teammates are, where opponents are on the field, or even when it is their turn to go in the game. Their performance goes down.

When athletes become stressed, there is an **increased fixation on the signs of stress**. They become focused on their bodies and the uncomfortable feelings of stress, and focusing on this makes the stress worse. By being focused on the stress in their bodies, athletes are not focused on the competition and their skills.

When athletes become stressed, there is a **decreased ability to tolerate pain and frustration**. All sports are very strenuous. All athletes have a time when their arms and legs "get heavy" or "burn" and it seems hard to go on. Being stressed hurries this fatigue and makes it harder to push through it. Great athletes have to be able to tolerate pain and fight the desire to "ease up." Stress makes this hard. Good sport psychology mental toughness skills help them succeed and get going when the going gets tough.

Stress leads to an **increased fixation on mistakes**. Mistakes always happen in a contest, but the key is to learn from them, make an adjustment, and move on. When athletes are stressed, they dwell on mistakes, get angry at themselves, and end up playing poorly. Being able to recover from a mistake is central to playing at a high level.

Stress leads to **decreased concentration**. Stress makes it harder to concentrate and to make decisions, especially split-second decisions. There can be "brain fade" and the mind going blank. This can lead to "freezing" and not reacting at a critical time. This focus on anxiety, and everything discussed above, leads to attention being directed away from where it should be for maximum performance.

Stress leads to "tunnel vision" and/ or "tunnel hearing." Under stress, an athlete's attention constricts and narrows; it is like being in a tunnel. Athletes do not see defenders coming or hear teammates calling. Keeping a flexible awareness of what is happening during a competition is essential. Stress creates a rigid narrow focus.

Finally, stress results in **mistakes and possible injury**. The decreased concentration results in more mistakes. The physical effects of stress, especially muscle tightness, can lead to injury. There is no athletic skill that is improved by tight muscles. Tightness decreases flexibility and coordination, and tight muscles are more subject to tears and other injuries.

CONTROLLING STRESS IN SPORT

There are many approaches to controlling stress in sport. In this section, we will briefly talk about some ways to help control the signs of stress described above. There are many approaches to promoting "relaxation" in the body. Remember though, that being relaxed is not for everyone. The key is for your athlete to switch on her ESP, for your athlete to be in her O-ZONE, whether that is relaxed, a little pumped up, or intensely activated.

This is really about self-regulation. We talked about the techniques to "up-regulate" when more energy is needed. These are the techniques to "down-regulate" when more calmness is desired.

Maybe you and your athlete are already aware of ways that athletes calm down when needed, or maybe there are some techniques that your athlete already uses. You and your athlete should write these in the spaces below:

WAYS THAT I OR OTHER ATHLETES CALM DOWN WHEN STRESSED

_____

_____

_____

_____

_____

_____

Some of the effective ways we know athletes down-regulate are listed and described below:

WAYS TO CONTROL COMPETITIVE STRESS

- **PERFORMANCE ENHANCING BREATHING TECHNIQUES**
- **CENTERING**
- **ATTENTION CONTROL TRAINING**
- **MEDITATION AND YOGA**
- **RELAXATION IMAGERY**
- **BIOFEEDBACK**

Performance-Enhancing Breathing Techniques

Breathing techniques are very effective approaches to managing stress during athletic contests. There are many forms and names for self-control breathing techniques. Whatever the name or specific form, slow rhythmic breathing shifts the body into a more relaxed state.

Diaphragmatic Breathing

Diaphragmatic Breathing is so called because it involves breathing anchored at the diaphragm, those muscles and tendons about half way down your athlete's upper body that separate the chest and abdominal cavity. It's considered a "deep" breathing technique.

You can introduce the idea of diaphragmatic breathing to your athlete in this manner. Tell your athlete that when you count to three, she should take the quickest, deepest breath possible and hold it for two seconds, exhale, and then return to normal breathing.

Next ask your athlete what she noticed (and you probably noticed, too) when this was done. If your athlete is like most athletes, she will report that she saw and felt her upper body, especially chest and shoulders rise up and be held in a tight position until breathing out. This is "chest breathing." If you ask your athlete what emotion this state looked and felt like, the answer will probably be surprise, fear, or stress. Chest breathing, especially in highly stressful competitive situations, can become uncomfortable and promote further stress. Diaphragmatic breathing is the opposite of this.

When your athlete "chest breathes," you will see her chest rise and fall, but with diaphragmatic breathing it is the stomach that expands and contracts. Diaphragmatic breathing tends to occur naturally when lying on your back. From that position, have your athlete observe whether her stomach rises and falls, rather than his or her chest. You may be aware that singers use this powerful technique of diaphragmatic breathing to enhance projection and endurance when performing.

You can help your athlete to develop and practice diaphragmatic breathing in this manner:
Tell her to
- Position one hand, palm down, on her stomach and the other hand, palm down, on the chest. If she is chest breathing, you will see the hand on her chest rise and fall. With diaphragmatic breathing, the hand on her stomach will rise and fall.
- Now have your athlete try to breathe deeply and slowly from the diaphragm. Notice the stomach distend, and the hand on the stomach rise and fall
- This can be helped along by having your athlete form her lips together like breathing through a straw. This helps produce diaphragmatic breathing
- Have your athlete also try taking little "sips" of air, as this can also promote diaphragmatic breathing

Diaphragmatic breathing may feel odd or uncomfortable, at first. This is normal. It will become easier, more effective, and more natural with practice and time. Also recognize that diaphragmatic breathing is not done all the time. It is used when needed. Your athlete can use this form of performance enhancing breathing in different ways.

Whenever your athlete starts to notice that she is becoming stressed, taking *one or two* diaphragmatic breaths can break the cycle of increasing stress (again, your athlete does not need to do diaphragmatic breathing all the time; only one or two breaths should be needed to work).

Your athlete can also develop a habit of taking one or two diaphragmatic breaths at various intervals during training, competition, or events. This can help remind your athlete to monitor her stress levels and mental focus. It can also provide an "automatic reset" of any stress that might be starting. This can prevent distortions in breathing during stress, which results in an imbalance of oxygen and carbon dioxide in the body and leads to feelings of uneasiness and even panic. Performance-enhancing breathing techniques counteract this.

Four-Count Method of Stress Control Breathing

Another form of performance enhancing breathing was recommended by a friend of ours, retired Army Ranger Lt. Colonel Dave Grossman. It is called the "4-count method." This technique is done by having your athlete breathe in through the nose to a slow count of 4, hold the breath for a count of 4, and then exhale slowly through the mouth for a count of 4. The cycle concludes by holding empty for another count of four. It goes like this:

In through the nose, two, three, four …

Hold, two, three, four …

Out through the lips, two, three, four …

Hold, two, three, four …

How slowly or quickly your athlete holds each count depends upon her comfort level and what works best. Like diaphragmatic breathing, the 4-count technique can be used to prevent or reduce stress. It can be repeated as necessary, but your athlete does not need to, nor should she do it all the time.

Performance-enhancing breathing techniques, like diaphragmatic breathing, are useful not only because of their effectiveness, but also because they are easy to do and can be done "covertly" in a variety of situations. In other words, your athlete can control and relax herself without anyone else being aware of it. However, once you and your athlete become aware of this powerful technique you may start to notice how many good athletes do this. You will notice pitchers taking a diaphragmatic breath before the pitch, basketball players before a foul shot, archers before release, and on and on.

> **The greatest efforts in sports comes when
> the mind is as still as a glass lake.**
>
> **-Timothy Gallwey
> Author, "Inner Game" Books**

Centering

Centering is another self-regulation technique that comes from the martial arts. It is well described by performance expert, Dr. Robert Nideffer (1975, 1978), who learned it while studying the martial art of Aikido in Japan. It is very effective for high stress situations. The purpose of centering is to develop a controlled state of relaxed focus. This is what the Japanese experts call a "mind like still water."

It can be practiced in the following manner (only have your athlete close his or her eyes during the training of this technique when it is safe to do so). You can help your athlete develop this sport psychology mental toughness skill by telling her to:

- Position yourself standing with one leg forward, your legs about shoulder width apart and knees slightly bent (a typical karate stance)
- Breathe in slowly and deeply just like a diaphragmatic breath
- Breathe out slowly and gently let your eyes close
- As you breathe out, gently let all your attention float down to a point in front of your waist at your "center of gravity." (The center of gravity is located about two inches behind the belly button, and this is the point where the body is most balanced.) This means that as your eyes close, let all your awareness focus in front of your bellybutton.
- Open your eyes and return to your regular breathing and activity

Sometimes it is hard for young athletes (or any athlete) to understand the idea of "letting attention" focus near the center of gravity. So you can also help your athlete to master Centering by adding a more familiar image, like a floating leaf or feather. Centering in this manner can be practiced by telling your athlete to:

- Position yourself standing with one leg forward, legs about shoulder width apart, and knees slightly bent
- Breathe in slowly and deeply just like a diaphragmatic breath
- Breathe out slowly and gently close your eyes as you imagine a leaf or feather floating slowly, slowly drifting down… lower and lower… until it gently comes to rest, floating softly at your belly button
- Open your eyes and return to your regular breathing and activity

Attention Control Training or ACT

Attention Control Training or ACT is a technique also developed by Dr. Nideffer. As used here, it combines diaphragmatic breathing, centering, and self-instruction.

Attention Control Training can be used by your athlete in several situations. It can be used:
(1) if something unexpected occurs that disrupts your athlete's attention and focus,
(2) if stress is building to uncomfortable levels for your athlete, or
(3) if a mistake occurred and it is distracting your athlete.

ACT is accomplished in the following way, much like centering. First, have your athlete take a slow, deep diaphragmatic breath. As your athlete exhales, have her focus her attention on breathing, and the feeling of calmness that is occurring. Immediately after exhaling, and while returning to normal breathing, have your athlete quietly say or think to herself a skill-related cue (word or phrase) to refocus on the competition. For example, your athlete might self-instruct by thinking or saying quietly "back to it," "speed," defend," "stay with her," or whatever leads to a successful refocus and readiness to play on.

ACT reduces distractions, creates calmness, and refocuses your athlete on the important aspects of the competition.

Meditation and Yoga

Meditation and Yoga are ancient Eastern techniques designed to control and quiet the body. At first they may seem strange to Americans & Westerners, however, they can be highly effective. In fact, it was the yogis and practitioners of these arts who "taught" Western Medicine that it is possible for an individual to control functions in the body that were believed to be only controllable by medication (heart rate, blood pressure, muscle tightness, skin temperature, even brain waves etc.). Meditation is based on concentrating or chanting a mantra, and yoga is based on rhythmic breathing techniques. Many community groups, YM or YWCA's, private studios, books, and tapes provide instruction on the many different forms of these self-regulation techniques.

More and more research is showing that there are significant performance enhancing benefits when individuals regularly practice meditation or yoga. Not only do these techniques produce calmness and confidence, they also seem to have positive cognitive effects. They seem to help the brain function more smoothly, decrease reaction times in certain situations, and do so with less mental fatigue, which provides longer and better concentration.

Relaxation Imagery

Relaxation Imagery is your athlete using her imagination to relax and feel calm when needed. We already discussed using imagery to psych up earlier, and we will discuss how to make imagery very effective in Chapter 8.

For now, you can help your athlete understand that the body responds to images that are in the brain. If your athlete fills her thoughts with pictures and images of pleasant, relaxing, happy scenes, this will help her feel that way. It will also help block any negative images or thoughts about performance.

While people often joke about going to their "happy place" to relax and feel calm, filling the mind with images of a favorite place does produce positive feelings. Sometimes, rather than thinking of a place, athletes will image a past performance where they felt really good, and they performed their best. They can then use those feelings to prepare mentally for the contest in which they are about to participate.

Biofeedback

Biofeedback is an approach that can use any relaxation technique, but tells your athlete if her body is getting relaxed. In biofeedback, a device is attached to an athlete's body that measures a physiological response that is related to stressed or relaxed states. Some examples are heart rate monitors, blood pressure monitors, brain wave monitors, "sweat reactions," or skin temperature.

For example, ask yourself and your athlete this: when athletes get nervous or stressed, does their finger skin temperature go up or down?" If you answered, down and colder, you are right. Think about the "cold sweat" that people get when they are nervous or stressed, a condition of cold clammy hands. Warmer hand and finger skin temperature is associated with relaxation and reduced stress. So, as an example, with biofeedback, athletes might learn to raise or maintain their skin temperature, because it is not possible to be stressed and relaxed at the same time. They learn to maintain or raise their skin temperature as a way to block stress reactions and stay calm. While athletes practice their favorite relaxation or self-regulation technique, the biofeedback device gives them feedback on whether their body is responding, and how much. Your athlete can learn to prevent, minimize, or reverse the effects of competitive stress by self-regulating his or her physiology.

There are some commercial simple biofeedback devices available, but if you and your athlete decide you wish to learn self-regulation by biofeedback, we would suggest first seeking out a sport psychologist with this expertise.

Progressive Muscle Relaxation (PMR)

There are many forms of effective muscle relaxation techniques, which not only reduce muscle tension, but also create a state of calmness. The emphasis here will be on Progressive Muscle Relaxation (PMR), for experience shows that it is effective, and easily and successfully used by athletes. In fact, while it often takes non-athletes many practice sessions to get an effect, in our experience, athletes often notice a good effect and relaxation from the first time they try it.

PMR has some other advantages over other relaxation techniques as well. It is an active approach, which fits in well with the action-orientation of athletes. It provides a good point of focus and concentration. It has been demonstrated to be superior to other techniques. And finally, while the initial training session may take up to fifteen minutes to complete, once the technique is mastered, the effects can be created in a matter of minutes, if not seconds.

PMR has its roots in the work of Dr. Edmund Jacobson, in the 1920's. It is a rather simple technique that has had good results. It involves first tensing, and then relaxing different muscle groups in the body. For example, the procedure begins with relaxing muscles in the hands and arms, proceeds to the shoulders and neck, further progresses to the chest, stomach, legs and into the toes.

How does PMR work? Tensing and relaxing the muscles trains them to relax and release tension. Reducing tension in the muscles creates good relaxation by itself. However, when muscles relax, other parts of the body also respond. Heart rate slows, blood pressure decreases, and breathing becomes slower and easier.

Training in PMR also helps athletes to recognize signs of tension in their muscles. Whether from stress or position, or both, it is important to become aware of muscle tension as soon as possible. Initiating relaxation at the earliest signs of muscle tension makes it easier to reverse the tension (rather than waiting until tension is really high and muscles are really tense).

Finally, the major way relaxation works, and why your athlete can learn to create it within a matter of seconds, is because of the "psychological conditioning" that takes place when your athlete adds a cue or command word to the process. This cue or command is a word or phrase that your athlete thinks or says to herself while practicing the muscle relaxation portion of PMR.

This cue can be any word or phrase that she likes, as long as it suggests relaxation, concentration and confidence. Words like "focus," "smooth," "easy," "ready," or even "relax," are fine. In other settings for relaxation, words like Hawaii or Blue Sky are often used to help create calmness. However, it's probably best that your athlete is not thinking about Hawaii or blue skies in the middle of a competition, so she should choose a cue word that fits better with the action of her sport.

With practice and training, by focusing on the cue or command word while your athlete creates control and relaxation by doing the muscle tension-relaxation, she is also "conditioning" or creating an association between the cue word and the state of relaxation. So, with practice, just thinking about the cue word will be the "sign" for the relaxation to start. Your athlete won't have to spend twenty minutes tensing muscles to achieve relaxation. A bit like flipping on a light switch, the conditioning will allow the switching on of relaxation when your athlete thinks of the cue or command word.

There are many potential benefits to your athlete learning a muscle relaxation technique. These include:

- **BETTER CONTROL OVER THE PHYSIOLOGY OF STRESS**
- **REDUCED COMPETITION STRESS AND ANXIETY**
- **IMPROVED CONCENTRATION AND FOCUS**
- **REDUCED CHANCE OF INJURY**
- **IMPROVED GENERAL STRESS REISISTANCE**
- **ENHANCED LEARNING AND SKILL ACQUISITION**

The main benefit of mastering self-regulation of competitive stress is to allow **control over the physiology of stress**. When that stress is physical, PMR can help manage and reduce it. But PMR can also prevent the negative effects of stress on thinking. A clear, relaxed state can facilitate thinking, concentration, and prevent brain lockdown. A relaxed state can reduce the likelihood of injury. When muscles are tight, there is a greater likelihood of a strain or tear. While we are focusing on the applications of PMR as related to competitive sport, it is important to realize that PMR, like most of the techniques we describe, not only help learning and performance in sport, but also in many areas of life.

There are some cautions in training relaxation. First, mastering relaxation and creating effective conditioning takes practice, just as any other athletic skill. Practice is necessary to both develop and maintain relaxation effects. Secondly, relaxation is a fundamental skill. It is not a cure-all or substitute for other skill training. Your athlete has to be smart about the application of relaxation training, especially if he or she becomes very good at producing relaxation. Use caution that your athlete does not create excessive relaxation before or during a competition. Too much relaxation can reduce performance in some athletic events. While it is unlikely that this would happen, remember, your athlete's goal is to be at her O-ZONE, and in her ESP.

Finally, relaxation techniques are almost always without "side effects." However, if your athlete has a psychological or health concern, it is best to check with your physician before intensely pursuing relaxation or other forms of psychological training. This is especially true should there be a history of psychological trauma.

We usually suggest that athletes seek guidance in such techniques, at least initially, from a competent sport psychologist. A further benefit from working with a sport psychologist is that there are other effective performance enhancing techniques that build on and mix the types of skills we discussed in more sophisticated approaches. For example, Visuo-Motor-Behavior-Rehearsal and Stress Inoculation Training are two powerful techniques that can be taught by the sport psychologist. So, there are many publicly available relaxation books and audio programs, but professional guidance should be considered. These techniques, when practiced and mastered, can help make your athlete a mentally tough and "unshakable" competitor.

VII
FAST AND FOCUSED:
CONCENTRATION SKILLS

...concentration and mental toughness are the margin of victory

-Bill Russell
Boston Celtics Center
11-time NBA Champion / 5-time MVP

The brain has incredible capability. For example, can you and your athlete read the following?

THE BRIAN IS TRLUY AMZAING AND CAN OFETN QUCIKLY SOVLE PRBOELMS AND SEEM TO MAKE SNESE OUT OF NOHTNIG.

WTIH JUST MNIMIAL CUES, LIKE THE FISRT AND LSAT LEETTR OF A WROD BEING IN PALCE, THE BRAIN CAN CRORETCLY FILL IN THE RSET. THIS IS BCEAUSE WE DO NOT RAED EACH LEETTR, BUT THE WROD AS A WHOLE.

STERSS CAN RELLAY FUOL UP ABIILTY, HWOVEER.

While the brain can make sense out of little, it is also sensitive to disruption by stress. That is why concentration is so critical, yet sensitive in sport. We turn once again to performance expert Dr. Robert Nideffer who said:

It's the ability to control attention under pressure and in response to changing demands that separates the average person from the super performer.

A lack of concentration leads to mistakes, errors and disappointing results. Concentration is the ability of your athlete to direct and maintain thought and attention.

Ask your athlete if the following are true or false:

TRUE OR FALSE?

1. **CONCENTRATION IS AN AUTOMATIC REFLEX**

2. **CONCENTRATION CAN NOT BE LEARNED**

3. **BECAUSE WE CONCENTRATE DAILY, PRACTICE IS NOT NEEDED**

4. **CONCENTRATION REQUIRES LITTLE ENERGY**

5. **OUR LEVEL OF CONCENTRATION ALWAYS FITS THE SITUATION**

All of the above statements are false.

While it occurs in everyday life, this does not mean that our concentration is getting trained, or that it is as strong as it might be. Concentration abilities are not fully automatic, and they can and need to be maximized. Daily use does not create the type of intense concentration needed in high level sport competition.

We all have the ability to concentrate. Your athlete has probably focused so intently on TV, music, a videogame (or school work?) that he or she didn't even hear you talking (or yelling!) to him or her. Concentration takes much energy, and can be quite tiring. And, often there is a mismatch between the degree of concentration needed in a situation, and our ability to engage in it. Concentration can be trained, strengthened, and improved, but it takes work and practice. It also takes great effort and energy to maintain concentration for an entire game, meet, or match.

You might often hear an athlete say: "I made a stupid mistake." We don't believe in that. Athletes aren't stupid, but they can let their concentration fade, and this is what is meant by the "stupid mistake." When an athlete says "I didn't know it was happening", or "I can't believe it happened," or "I guess I wasn't thinking," he is saying that concentration was not what is should have been.

> **My concentration was at such a high level.**
> **My mind was right there.**
> **I felt fresh, like I could stop everything.**
>
> **- Patrick Roy after winning the Stanley Cup**

There are some aspects to concentration that are important for your athlete to be aware of when training and competing. A very important aspect is the breadth, or width of focus.
Concentration can either be very narrow and pinpoint, or it can be very broad and wide-range.

If you and your athlete think about it, you will both recognize that some sports, and sport skills, require an athlete to be very narrowly focused, while other sports and skills are performed best when attention takes in the whole field or situation. In the space below, can you write in different sports or skills that require either a narrow focus or a broad focus?

SPORTS AND SKILLS NEEDING DIFFERENT TYPES OF FOCUS

PINPOINT/ NARROW

_____

_____

_____

_____

_____

_____

BROAD/WIDE-RANGE

_____

_____

_____

_____

_____

_____

If you weren't sure about this, you and your athlete can check on the following page for some examples of sports and skills that require different types of focus. If you are sure, or have checked out the next page, it will now be helpful to think about what kinds of specific skills in your athlete's sport are performed best with different types of concentration and focus. Write them in the space below.

SPECIFIC SKILLS IN MY SPORT NEEDING DIFFERENT TYPES OF FOCUS

PINPOINT/ NARROW

_____

_____

_____

_____

_____

_____

BROAD/WIDE-RANGE

_____

_____

_____

_____

_____

_____

Here are some examples of sports and skills performed best with different types of focus:

SPORT SKILLS/ POSITIONS NEEDING DIFFERENT TYPES OF FOCUS

PINPOINT/ NARROW	BROAD/ WIDE-RANGE
Archery - Bull's-eye	Football – Quarterback
Baseball - Pitching	Basketball- Point Guard
Weight Lifting –Bench Press	Hockey – Goalie
Wrestling –Escape	Soccer – Sweeper
Golf-Putting	

Let's assume your athlete's specific sport is soccer. Examples of SOCCER skills needing different types of concentration are below:

SOCCER SKILLS NEEDING DIFFERENT TYPES OF FOCUS

PINPOINT/ NARROW	BROAD/ WIDE-RANGE
Receiving the ball	Reading defense before a pass
Penalty Kick	Tracking runs on a corner kick
Saving a Shot	Assuring everyone is marked on restart

The purpose of thinking about different types of focus is for your athlete to decide if he is able to do the kind of concentration that a particular skill requires, and /or to begin to think about developing the best type of concentration skill for the kind of skills he will need in competition.

The wrong type of concentration leads to poor performance. For example, if your athlete is preparing to play a through-ball to a streaking teammate, and fails to recognize the defender anticipating the pass, the ball will likely be intercepted. Focusing on the target alone is too narrow, as the defender is likely using a broad focus to respond to the play.

However, if your athlete is really aware about concentration and his sport, you might correctly hear:

Hey, my sport often requires BOTH types of focus.

And that would be correct. Your athlete is exactly right that many times there is the need to be able to **SHIFT** attention very quickly between a narrow and broad focus in order to play the best.

In fact, there are three aspects to concentration in sport, and three questions that your athlete should ask to determine whether or not his focus is as disciplined as it should be. These are:

DIMENSIONS OF CONCENTRATION IN SPORT
&
THREE ESSENTIAL QUESTIONS ABOUT THEM

INTENSITY: CAN I CONCENTRATE HARD ENOUGH?

DURATION: CAN I CONCENTRATE LONG ENOUGH?

FLEXIBILITY: CAN I SHIFT MY ATTENTION AS NEEDED?

The first dimension is *intensity,* and the question your athlete should ask himself is whether in any given situation *"Can I concentrate hard enough?"*

The second dimension is *duration,* and the question your athlete should ask himself is whether in any given situation *"Can I concentrate long enough?"*

The third dimension is *flexibility,* and the question your athlete should ask himself is whether in any given situation *"Can I shift attention as I need to?"*

If your athlete cannot answer an emphatic "YES" to each of these questions, it may be a good idea to try to enhance his concentration and attention skills.

But first, let's do a quick test of your athlete's visual and scanning attention. One way to test your athlete's concentration is to have him complete the concentration grid found at the end of this book.

Numbers from 00 to 99 have been placed randomly in different spots on the grid. To assess your athlete's current ability to concentrate, time your athlete for one minute in searching for numbers in order. Give your athlete the grid face down, and when you say "go," have your athlete turn over the sheet and begin crossing out the numbers in order from 00 to 100, as quickly as possible, until you say "stop," one minute later.

That is, have your athlete look for and start with 00, then look for and cross out 01, then 02, 03, 04 and so forth, until one minute is up. Remember to cross out the numbers in order, and do not skip any in sequence. Go ahead and give it a try.

How did your athlete do? How many numbers were found and crossed off in one minute? On this exercise, made popular by famous sport psychologist Dr. Dorothy Harris, elite athletes are able to reach the mid to upper twenties in one minute. The highest score we ever obtained was 35, from a professional soccer goalkeeper.

Don't be discouraged, and don't let your athlete be discouraged, if the score was not that high. First, remember the scores we are citing are from elite Olympic and Professional athletes. Secondly, the idea is to use this as a challenge to build the strength of your athlete's concentration.

Some athletes use this type of concentration grid to help strengthen their attention skills. They practice with the grid by making up new forms that have the numbers placed in different random orders. (A random number generator on a computer can help with this). With practice, athletes try to get further and further in one minute.

There is another approach, called the **FOCUSING PRACTICE TECHNIQUE,** which your athlete can use to build concentration. This is done by picking an object and having your athlete focus on it as intensely and as long as possible.

We suggest that your athlete choose an object related to his sport. For example, a good focus object might one of the practice baseballs or softballs (for ballplayers). In a quiet room, have your athlete sit and look at the ball. Have your athlete try to notice everything possible about it. Focus on the color. Focus on the texture. Is it smooth, are there nicks or tears? Are there places where it is faded? Are there different shadings on it? How does light reflect off of it or illuminate it? Follow the stitching.

The key is for your athlete stay focused on the ball as long as possible and not to be distracted by anything else. As important, is being aware of and avoiding mind "drift" because your athlete gets bored. If your athlete tells you that during the session his mind is on "why am I doing this stuff," or that it is "weird," this is an indication that mental discipline is not as strong as it might be. Have your athlete try to keep focus on the ball a little longer at each practice session. You can start with a session of about 15 seconds, and when concentration can be successfully maintained that long, you can increase the concentration time to 30 seconds, then 45, and up to, but no longer than, two minutes.

The other important aspect to maximizing your athlete's attention with this technique is to begin to introduce distractions. For example, after focusing in a quiet room, turn on the radio or music very low. Have your athlete try not to listen to the music, but maintain focus on the ball. Try to have your athlete not even hear the music. We like to suggest using talk radio as the distraction. If focused well, your athlete should not even hear or remember anything that was said on the radio. Then, with each practice session, turn the music or talk up a little louder. Keep progressing until focus can be maintained, even with a strong distraction.

Another excellent way to enhance this training is to make a tape of the sounds of the crowd and other noises at one of your athlete's actual competitions. Then, use this tape in the drill, slowly making it louder, and increasing the potential distraction, while your athlete stays focused on the object.

When your athlete is able to concentrate well in this setting, have your athlete do this drill in a more realistic setting. Eventually, do the drill in the sport setting, that is, the field, track, pool, gym, etc.

This approach trains attention to strengthen focus, which is often the hardest thing to do in highly charged sport contests. But, as noted before, too much of a narrowed focus is not a good thing. So, the above exercise can be used to train attention flexibility and broadening, as well.

Using the same approach as above, have your athlete begin shifting attention from the focus object (baseball) to the distraction. For example, if your athlete is using radio music or talk show dialogue as a distraction, have him practice shifting attention back to the music or talk, and ignore the focus object. Then shift back to the focus object.

Another opportunity to practice auditory concentration is anytime your athlete is in a crowded room where there are multiple conversations occurring. Your athlete can use a situation like this to strengthen attention by variously concentrating on all the sounds in the setting. By "scanning," and consciously listening to all aspects of what is going on around them, your athlete can develop this shifting and acute awareness as a skill. Have your athlete pick out one sound or conversation on which to focus, but then switch to other conversations or sounds. Switch between single specific conversations or sounds and the whole din of the setting. Go from narrow, to broad, and back.

One last technique that is fun and can be effective involves your athlete listening to his favorite music, but compartmentalizing the sounds and instruments that are heard. When listening to favorite songs, have your athlete try to notice melody lines, or instrumental riffs, that may have not been obvious before. Have your athlete try to focus away from the words or main melody and focus, say, on the bass or piano. See if it is possible to pick out the bass line or drum rhythms and enjoy them while excluding the more obvious melody or words on which your athlete usually focuses. Have your athlete move back and forth between a narrow intense focus to a broad comprehensive one of all the sounds that are present.

With practice your athlete should find it easier to stay focused and intense during competitions. Using the information from the previous exercise, where your athlete described the skills that need a broad or narrow focus as a guide, he should be better able to prepare and practice applying the best type of focus for that moment of performance. Your athlete should get better at paying attention to what is important during the game and ignoring distractions that will interfere with a best *focused* effort.

There are various computer-based concentration-training programs, but they can be rather expensive. Some computer games and systems can help strengthen focus when use appropriately.

VIII
INSTANT PREPLAY:
PERFORMANCE-ENHANCING IMAGERY

Imagery...is the most important of the mental skills
required for winning the mind game in sports.

-Dr. Shane Murphy
Former Head
Sport Psychology Department
U.S. Olympic Committee

One of the most powerful sport psychology mental toughness techniques is mental imagery. Mental imagery has a long history in sport and all human performance. Mental imagery, or mental practice as it is sometimes called, is when your athlete imagines performance in her mind.

In one survey, ninety percent of the athletes and ninety-four percent of the coaches, surveyed at the United States Olympic Training Center, reported that they used imagery in training for their sport. Ninety-seven percent of the athletes and one hundred percent of the coaches agreed that imagery enhances performance.

Almost everyone has experienced mental imagery to some degree at one time or another. Maybe your athlete was invited to a party, and imagined how much fun it would be, or perhaps there was a reluctance to go, because of imagery that portrayed how boring the party would be. What your athlete was thinking, thoughts and images in her mind probably affected her attitude towards going to a great degree.

Or, perhaps your athlete had to give a speech and "imagined" giving the talk, how it went, and how people responded. Whether your athlete imaged doing well or doing poorly probably had a big impact on how confident she felt before giving that speech.

Perhaps the best example of the power of imagery to affect us is in reading or listening to a story. We have all experienced how words can conjure up pictures as we listen. We all know how scary or heart-warming a book can be, and how it can make us feel really frightened, creepy, or warm and fuzzy. These are all examples of how imagery can affect performance. In sport it is especially powerful.

There are some keys that separate performance-enhancing imagery in sport from everyday imagination, and make imagery very effective for improved performance. These are listed below:

HOW TO MAKE PERFORMANCE ENHANCING IMAGERY EFFECTIVE

> **IMAGE IN ALL FIVE SENSES**

> **USE THE BEST PERSPECTIVE**

> **PRACTICE THE IMAGERY**

> **IMAGE CORRECT RESPONSES**

> **IMAGE IN REAL TIME**

> **IMAGE PROBLEMS & OVERCOMING THEM**

> **USE MOVEMENT AND KINESTHETIC IMAGERY**

Imagery becomes much more effective when the images of your athlete's performance involve **all five senses**. Many athletes just think about what they "see" when they image their performance. Imagery will be more effective if your athlete images not only what he sees when competing, but also what is heard, felt (both touch and emotions), tasted, and smelled.

Often times you will hear the term "visualization" used to describe performance-enhancing imagery. (You will see it used in many of the quotes from famous athletes here in this book). We don't like this term, however, because it implies that athletes should just "see" with their imagination. Imagery should use all five of the senses to make it as real as possible, and to help transfer it from your athlete's mind to the actual competition.

Some senses, like seeing, hearing, and feeling may be easier to image than others (taste and smell). With practice, however, your athlete should be able to improve imagery in all the senses. It is not necessary to have strong imagery in every sense for it to be useful. Seeing, hearing, and feeling are probably most important.

Below is an exercise to help your athlete assess how easy it is for her to image in different senses, and to begin practicing imagery. It is rather general, and you will want to construct a similar exercise specific to your athlete's sport.

Read the following to your athlete, and have her try to follow the directions below as best as possible. Pause for few seconds between each image suggestion.

USING YOUR MENTAL SENSE OF VISION, SEE

THE COLORS OF YOUR JERSEY....
THE LINES ON THE FIELD....
BLEACHERS FILLED WITH FRIENDS AND FANS...

USING YOUR MENTAL SENSE OF HEARING, LISTEN TO

THE STARTING WHISTLE FOR THE GAME....
THE CROWD CHEERING YOU ON....
THE COACH SHOUTING INSTRUCTIONS....

USING YOUR MENTAL SENSE OF TOUCH, FEEL

YOUR MUSCLES GIVING YOU SPEED....
THE RELEASE OF THE BALL....
SWEAT RUNNING DOWN YOUR FACE....
THE EXCITEMENT OF GOOD PLAY....

USING YOUR MENTAL SENSE OF TASTE, TASTE

YOUR MOUTH DRY AND THIRSTY....
THE COOLNESS OF SPORTS DRINK....

USING YOUR MENTAL SENSE OF SMELL, SMELL

THE FRESH CUT GRASS....
YOUR CLEATS IN THE LOCKER OR GYM...
YOUR CLEATS *AFTER A WEEK* IN YOUR BAG !...

How did your athlete do? Remember if your athlete had some difficulty getting all the images clear, practice will help her improve and refine imagery skills. Your athlete may want to practice imagery with the example you prepared, or develop her own imagery descriptions. Please remember, the above is a drill to work with imagery as a skill, not specific suggestions on what to image or concentrate on at a competition.

The second key to making imagery effective is the **PERSPECTIVE** or viewpoint your athlete uses when doing imagery. To help your athlete discover and understand the different perspectives, ask her to do the following:

For the next 10 seconds, close your eyes and image yourself playing, (or performing or competing....). Do that now.

Then discuss with your athlete what the imagery was like. If your athlete was watching herself from the distance as in a view from the stands this is called the **"THIRD PERSON"** or **"EXTERNAL PERSPECTIVE."** This is a viewpoint where your athlete is an observer watching herself from afar.

If your athlete's images were those that she actually sees when performing, this is called the **"FIRST PERSON"** or **"INTERNAL" PERSPECTIVE.** This is a viewpoint where your athlete experiences exactly what she perceives during a contest. The view is not that of an observer from the distance, but that of a participant, being directly engaged.

There is no solid information about which perspective is best for enhancing performance. Initial reports indicated that elite athletes tended to use internal/first person imagery. This made sense as this perspective is most like a real-life situation. However, later research found that the perspective used did not correlate with performance and being selected for elite teams. Further, other reports about Olympic athletes note that 17 to 35 percent use internal/first person imagery; 30 to 39 percent use external/third person imagery and 34 to 44 percent use both (Morris, Spittle, & Watt, 2005).

Personal experience in working with athletes, and in other areas of elite human performance, has engendered our preference for the internal/first person perspective. We believe that the more realistic view is ultimately more preparatory and effective. There is research that also supports this. However, since both perspectives can be effective, your athlete should use the view that is most comfortable and works the best in terms of performance.

Your athlete may want to consider using both perspectives. One approach that makes sense is to begin by first using the external perspective, like watching a demonstration of the skill, and then follow it by imaging the performance of the skill or routine from the internal perspective. The third person/ external perspective has been said to be useful for observation, critiquing and when emotional distance is desired. The first person/ internal perspective has been said to be more powerful when an athlete wants to fully engage and feel the performance, both physically and emotionally.

The next key to maximizing the effectiveness of imagery is to have your athlete **practice** the performance-enhancing imagery. We will say this again: psychological skills for sport performance must be practiced just like physical skills. Practice not only improves your athlete's ability to image, but it also provides another form of practice for improving the physical skills being imaged.

It is essential that your athlete **image skills correctly**. Imagery is like practice, and if your athlete images skills sloppily or incorrectly, the brain-body connection will be conditioned to respond in this suboptimal way. If your athlete is not sure how to correctly perform a particular skill, be sure to check with her coach *before* practicing mentally to be sure the imagery of the form or execution of the skill is correct. The sayings that "you play the way you practice" and "Practice doesn't make perfect, *perfect practice* makes perfect" are true for your athlete's psychological, as well as, physical skills.

It is also important for your athlete to **image skills in real time**, or at the speed at which the skill, play, or routine will actually occur. Just like when your athlete first learns a new physical skill, it is ok to image it more slowly initially, but ultimately the imagery of the skills should be at the same speed at which they are performed.

It is essential to always have your athlete image performing well and being successful. However, it is also essential to have your athlete **image problems, and how to overcome them.** It is ok, and actually good, to image problems like a false start, being further behind than expected in a relay race, or being down by a goal in the closing minutes of a game. However, it is crucial to always have your athlete image how that situation will be managed. Your athlete should image how she will recover from a setback, how intensity will be maintained or increased, or what new tactics might be employed. Help your athlete learn to use imagery to anticipate, prevent, or overcome possible problems.

Finally, just because imagery is a psychological and mental toughness technique, it does not mean that your athlete has to engage in it while lying on a couch or sitting still. In fact, it is good to **use movement and engage in kinesthetic imagery.** The performance enhancing effects of imagery are increased if your athlete gently mimics or pantomimes the skill, play, or routine while imaging it. Certainly part of the imagery should be the (kinesthetic) physical feel of the movement. Have your athlete merge movement and imagery for maximum effect.

In sport, mental imagery is used primarily to help you get the best out of yourself in training and competition. The developing athletes who make the fastest progress and those who ultimately become their best make extensive use of mental imagery. They use it daily as a means of directing what will happen in training, and as a way of pre-experiencing their best competition performances.

-Dr. Terry Orlick
Famous Canadian Sport Psychologist

Performance-enhancing imagery can play a big role in preparing your athlete for playing as best as possible. There are several ways performance-enhancing imagery can be used to do this. They include:

WAYS TO USE IMAGERY TO ENHANCE PERFORMANCE

➢ **IMPROVE A SPECIFIC SPORT SKILL**
➢ **ANALYZE AND CORRECT ERRORS**
➢ **PREPARE FOR COMPETITION**
➢ **ENHANCE CONFIDENCE**

Imagery can be used when your athlete wants to **learn a new skill or improve a specific skill.** Imagery is another way to practice skills. Think of it as an extra practice session that your athlete can do almost anytime, even if it is not possible to get to the track, court, mat, or field. Sport psychology research shows that mentally practicing a skill can improve actual physical performance, because when athletes image a certain skill, very small electrical impulses occur in the muscles of the part of the body they are thinking about. This means that the brain is making connections between itself and the muscles, just like in physical practice.

Imagery can also be used for **analyzing mistakes and making corrections**. Sometimes if a competition didn't go well, it is useful for your athlete to "replay" the game or routine in imagery. Very often your athlete will discover the point where he or she was unsure, or where skills were not executed as they should have been. It is important for your athlete to then image those actions or events again with the *correct or improved* performance, so that the images of the mistake are "erased" and replaced by images of desired performance. Your athlete does not want the residue of suboptimal performance images lingering in her brain. "Record over" that performance with mental editing for improved and maximized performance.

Imagery can also be used to catch mistakes before they occur. Your athlete should be able to see the execution of a skill, play, move, or routine in imagery exactly as he wants it to occur at the competition. If your athlete cannot image her skill or routine flawlessly, she is probably not in optimal readiness to perform it in actual competition. Imagery can help your athlete find points where he or she may be confused or unsure of what to do, and train-up the skill before it is needed.

Imagery can be used to **prepare for competition and specific situations.** Athletes can use imagery to prepare how to defend her assigned opponent, manage the frustration of being in the penalty box, at what point in the race to begin the kick, how to ride the wave that is bigger and stronger than expected, or how to "sizzle their pits" (ask a volleyball player).

Your athlete can practice what to do in any given situation. With imagery, your athlete can prepare for any situation that might be encountered, even if it is not possible to physically practice for it. For example, wet weather, windy weather, darkness closing in, having a key player miss the game at the last moment, and other similar situations can be addressed before they need an immediate response. Having at least seen and practiced a response to a difficult, unexpected, or stressful situation in mental training, your athlete will know what to try when it occurs in the game or competition.

Finally, imagery can be used to **enhance your athlete's confidence**. Actually, just by practicing imagery, confidence can improve. By practicing different kinds of situations, and knowing what strategy will be used in them, confidence increases due to enhanced feelings of readiness. Remember that a big part of stress is feeling unprepared. Imagery can enhance the feelings of preparation and readiness for your athlete.

Your athlete can also use imagery more directly to enhance or restore confidence, by imaging past games or competitions where he or she performed very well and was very successful. If your athlete images these past successes in all five senses, not only will her body feel the good sensations of physical performance, it will also feel the emotions of confidence that went with that performance. If your athlete's confidence needs a boost this is a great way to build it back up quickly.

Your athlete can merge performance-enhancing imagery into their competitive preparations in a variety of ways. Generally, it is good to make it part of pre-competition preparation. On the way to the competition, in the locker room, or while warming up, your athlete can image various aspects of the contest. Some athletes sit and close their eyes and image for several minutes. Other athletes do this briefly, with their eyes open, and move while doing so.

Your athlete can quickly image a skill before any special situation. Brief imagery, while in the starting blocks, at a face-off, or tip-off, can focus energy for an explosive start, strong push off the ball or puck, or maximum vertical jump. Imagery can be a powerful psychological technique to move your athlete's skill and confidence to the next level.

By the way, perhaps you or your athlete were wondering how just "thinking about something" results in improved physical performance. The short answer has two parts. First, as we already discussed, imagery allows your athlete to prepare for unexpected situations, so that when they do occur, the reaction can be more immediate and appropriate. As important, is that, because of advanced diagnostic techniques like brain scans (fMRI) or near-infrared spectroscopy (NIRS), we now know that when athletes image a skill, it activates the same parts of the brain and same brain-body connections as if the skill were actually being performed physically. Not magic, but neuroscience.

IX
CHAMPIONSHIP THINKING:
SELF-TALK AND OPTIMAL PERFORMANCE

I've always believed that you can think positive just as well as you can think negative.

-Sugar Ray Robinson
ESPN's Greatest Boxer in History
Boxing Hall of Fame

You hear it all the time:

"Think Positive!" "Be Positive!"

But how does your athlete do that? Where does that positive attitude come from? Much of it stems from how athletes "talk" to themselves. For most people, thinking feels like having a conversation with themselves. This is called self-talk. While some people think more in pictures, most people and athletes talk to themselves a great deal.

What your athlete says to himself has a BIG impact on his feelings and performance. Before athletes do anything, or feel anything, they say something to themselves. While most of the time they are not aware of their self-talk, it is there. When athletes think and engage in self-talk that is confident, encouraging, and skill oriented, they will perform at their best. If athletes think negative, angry, or worrying thoughts, they are primed to have a subpar performance. The good news is that athletes can become aware of their self-talk, and when they do, they can change it in ways that maximize performance.

While "thinking positive" is often emphasized in sport, there is something even more important than thinking positively, which is to **AVOID NEGATIVE THINKING.**

Actually the better way to say this (and we tell you why shortly) is to engage in **SKILL SPECIFIC SELF-TALK (SSST).**

Negative thinking can be so powerful in ruining effort and performance that it has been called **"stinkin' thinkin'."** Can you and your athlete think of some ways that negative thinking can degrade (your athlete's) performance. Write the ways in the spaces below:

HOW NEGATIVE THINKING AFFECTS MY PERFORMANCE

_____

_____

_____

_____

_____

_____

_____

Research and experience have found that negative thinking affects the quality of performance in these ways:

WAYS THAT NEGATIVE THINKING AFFECTS PERFORMANCE

- **IT REDUCES YOUR CONFIDENCE**

- **IT SETS YOU UP FOR FAILURE AND SELF-DOUBT**

- **IT DISTRACTS YOU AND DEGARDES YOUR CONCENTRATION**

- **IT SPREADS TO YOUR TEAMMATES**

- **IT SPREADS TO OTHER AREAS OF YOUR LIFE**

Negative thinking, through self-talk, affects athletes in many different ways. One very important effect is that negative self-talk **REDUCES SELF- CONFIDENCE**. It is hard for your athlete to feel good about his performance when negative self-messages are present. Thinking negatively can make your athlete worry about personal performance. It can create tension and anxiety. When your athlete's confidence is down, enthusiasm and spirit for winning suffers.

Negative thinking **SETS YOUR ATHLETE UP FOR DOUBT AND FAILURE.** It erases your athlete's belief in his ability to do well and succeed. It makes your athlete question how well he will be able to play. It also creates the expectation that your athlete will not do well, and expectations have a very powerful effect on behavior.

Negative thinking **DISTRACTS AND DEGARDES YOUR ATHLETE'S CONCENTRATION.** When your athlete's mind is filled with negative thoughts, focus is not on the game. Your athlete's focus is on something other than performance.

Negative thinking **SPREADS TO TEAMMATES**. Rather than being a model of enthusiasm for the team and helping to get everyone "psyched" for the game, meet, or tournament, negative thinking by your athlete can drag a team down. Negative thinking can distract teammates who are trying to focus on their own maximum effort.

Negative thinking **SPREADS TO OTHER AREAS OF YOUR ATHLETE'S LIFE**. Maybe the worst thing about negative thinking in sport is that negative thoughts can spread to other areas of your athlete's life: school, family, relationships. When your athlete starts dwelling on the negative in one area, he can start to do this all the time. Your athlete can start to lose belief in himself overall.

The great Minnesota Vikings quarterback Fran Tarkenton knew this when he said:

Negative attitudes are a sort of poison.

Because negative thinking is so powerful in a bad way, it is very important that your athlete try to avoid it in his sport (and life). Even though there is so much emphasis on thinking positively, we believe that *IT IS MORE IMPORTANT TO AVOID NEGATIVE SELF-TALK THAN TO ENGAGE IN POSITIVE SELF-TALK*. Why do we say this?

If you don't think you can . . . you won't.

-Jerry West
Los Angeles Lakers, Player & Coach
12-time NBA All-Star
Hall of Fame
Model for the NBA logo

First, negative thinking seems to have more of an impact on how an athlete performs than positive self-talk. If your athlete thinks or self-talks that he will do something, it can help achieve it. It can increase motivation. However, just telling himself that he will do something does not mean that it will surely happen. Other factors, not in your athlete's control, can affect the outcome or quality of his performance. However, **we can guarantee that telling yourself that you can't do something will keep you from doing it.** When your athlete says he can't, it's over.

Secondly, while we think positive self-talk can be helpful, the best type of self-talk is what we call being able to **STEP-UP**, which stands for **SELF-TALK for ENHANCED PERFORMANCE –UNDER PRESSURE.** This is a type of self-talk that focuses your athlete's attention on how to perform, and execute skills, not just wanting to do so. It is like having your athlete's coach shrink down in size and sit on your athlete's shoulder, whispering in his ear, and talking your athlete through the competition and performance.

> **My thoughts before a big race are usually pretty simple.**
> **I tell myself: "Get out of the blocks, run your race, stay relaxed.**
> **If you run your race, you'll win…Channel your energy. Focus."**
>
> **-Carl Lewis**
> Olympic Track Great
> 9 Gold Olympic Medals
> 8 Gold World Championship Medals

STEP-UP is comprised of "self-instructions" or coaching cues that are related to how to execute a skill, play, or routine. This is what we mean by **SSST or SKILL SPECIFIC SELF-TALK**. These are single words or short phrases that focus your athlete on *how* to perform his best. They are the words that the coach might use to focus on what to do to play well. An example for starting a race in swimming might be:

➢ **FOCUS**
➢ **EXPLODE**
➢ **STREAMLINE**
➢ **STRETCH**

Another example for sprinting at the finish might be:

➢ **NOW**
➢ **KICK HARD**
➢ **ACCELERATE TO THE WALL**

Notice that these are all words and phrases that instruct you on HOW to perform. Saying or thinking "I'll win" or "I'm going to do well" may get your athlete "up," but it doesn't tell your athlete HOW or WHAT TO DO to succeed. It is much like the famous Nike slogan of "Just do it." Very motivational, but just do WHAT? Success in sport and elite performance is about doing specific things (skills) very well, and very consistently. Just doing it, doesn't really do it. Your athlete's self-talk should focus on the process of how to perform and execute the skills needed at a given moment. This is SSST, Skill Specific Self-Talk.

Too many athletes focus on the goal or the outcome of their effort. Again, imaging the excitement of winning a game, or making the team, can be motivating, but it doesn't guide your athlete on how to make that happen. Wishing for the fastest time doesn't produce it. Performing your strokes perfectly, maintaining form, or squaring for a shot is how it happens and Self-Talk for Enhanced Performance, STEPPING-UP, is how you maximize your skill and performance.

How does your athlete train to STEP-UP? You can discuss the steps below with your athlete.

STEP-UP
DEVELOPING SELF-TALK FOR
ENHANCED PERFORMANCEUNDER STRESS

- **FIND YOUR O-ZONE**

- **CREATE YOUR ESP**

- **ENCOURAGE YOURSELF**

- **ENCOURAGE OTHERS**

- **MONITOR AND CHANGE NEGATIVE THOUGHTS**

- **USE SSST; SKILL SPECIFIC SELF-TALK**

- **PHRASE ALL SSST POSITIVELY**

STEP-UP is most easy to develop and use when your athlete understands and has identified his **O-ZONE,** and has mastered the skills necessary to **CREATE THE ENHANCED STATE FOR PERFORMANCE.** Your athlete should be in his ESP, as we discussed earlier in this manual. Being in the ESP indicates readiness and means both physical and psychological skills will be at their best.

> **Learn to think like a winner....**
> **Think positive and visualize your strengths.**
>
> **-Vic Braden**
> Tennis Player and Famed Instructor

STEP-UP develops most quickly, and stays the strongest, when your athlete learns to **ENCOURAGE HIMSELF.** Words like "dummy," "jerk," "loser," or worse, should never be part of your athlete's thinking or self-talk, even if there is a mistake, or performance is below what was expected and desired. Self-encouragement will pave the way to maximum performance for your athlete.

STEP-UP becomes stronger when your athlete also tries to **ENCOURAGE OTHERS**. It is important to support teammates. There are positive effects from appreciating the efforts of others, including your athlete's opponents. Some athletes seem to feel a need to "put-down" their competitors. This is often found in athletes who are unsure of themselves and lack self-confidence. They seek to increase their own self-esteem by criticizing others.

This is a big problem. First, confidence is best developed by the kinds of self-talk we are discussing and by performing well, not by demeaning others. Secondly, criticizing a mentally tough athlete will have no effect on him or her. It will only distract your athlete. Lastly, if your athlete develops the habit of putting down others, it can develop into a very negative style that can very easily turn on him.

STEP-UP is developed by your athlete **MONITORING FOR INSTANCES OF NEGATIVE SELF-TALK, AND CHANGING NEGATIVE STATEMENTS TO SSST, SKILL SPECIFIC SELF-TALK**. Your athlete can monitor his self-talk with the help of the self-talk monitoring chart which follows.

The chart has space for your athlete to write down the **SITUATION** where he catches any negative thinking and self-talk. This might be a good time for your athlete to review the situations that were listed as "stressful" back in Chapter 6, because these are instances when self-talk or negative thinking are likely to occur.

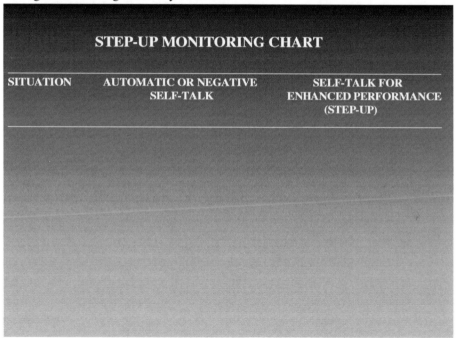

STEP-UP MONITORING CHART

SITUATION	AUTOMATIC OR NEGATIVE SELF-TALK	SELF-TALK FOR ENHANCED PERFORMANCE (STEP-UP)

It also provides space to write down your athlete's usual or **AUTOMATIC NEGATIVE SELF-TALK** in such situations. Finally, there is space for your athlete to write down more effective, **STEP-UP** words and phrases, which can substitute for the negative ones. This is where SSST should be developed.

The following are some examples of STEP-UP monitoring charts with situations that are potentially stressful for swimmers. Notice that for the stressful situations there are automatic negative self-talk. If you and your athlete read these automatic negative statements, we think you will both see that thinking like this will create more stress, anxiety, and degrade performance. The statements certainly will not lead to optimal performance or suggest how to get there. If you and your athlete read the statements in the STEP-UP column, however, we think both of you will see how they are skill specific self-talk and can help to keep an athlete focused by specific directions on how to perform at their personal best, even in a challenging situation.

STEP-UP MONITORING CHART

SITUATION	AUTOMATIC OR NEGATIVE SELF-TALK	SELF-TALK FOR ENHANCED PERFORMANCE (STEP-UP)
My main rival swims a personal best in the race before me	No way I can beat that time today. What's the point. I might as well just hang it up.	Focus. Crank it up for my best. Use my kick to my Advantage.

Now consider the following situation:

STEP-UP MONITORING CHART

SITUATION	AUTOMATIC OR NEGATIVE SELF-TALK	SELF-TALK FOR ENHANCED PERFORMANCE (STEP-UP)
I didn't get the lane I wanted.	I never get a break. I always swim slow in this lane. I wish I had an outside lane.	Forget superstitions. Focus on technique. Push it hard on my turns. Image my race.

You can help your athlete develop mentally tough self-talk by working with a STEP-UP self-monitoring chart, using examples from his sport. Have your athlete think of various situations that may be stressful. Have your athlete write them down one at a time and then write the automatic negative self-talk that occurred when the situation happened or would likely occur if the situation happened. Then have your athlete develop SSST, the alternate words or phrases to

STEP-UP and use instead of the negative ones. By anticipating such situations (or reviewing if they already happened) your athlete can practice and prepare to mange a tough situation before it occurs. Feeling prepared, and having a plan, not only provides needed action, it also reduces worry about the situation and builds confidence.

Remember STEP-UP is comprised of words and phrases that tell how to perform. The words and phrases should be short and related to the skill that your athlete wants to execute.
It is perfectly fine, and actually a good idea, to discuss the STEP-UP self-instructions and phrases with the coach.

STEP-UP works best when your athlete learns to **PHRASE ALL SSST IN THE POSITIVE,** which is, stating *what to do* in the situation. You athlete should avoid stating *what not to do* **in the situation.**

For example, if in track, your athlete's starts are too slow, avoid self-instruction like "DON'T BE SO SLOW." Rather, use SSST phrases like, "BURST OUT OF THE BLOCKS" OR "STRETCH IT OUT."

Another example from soccer might be that your athlete struggles with penalty kick placement (like shooting penalty kicks too high over the cross bar). It is best to avoid STEP-UP instruction like "DON'T SHOOT HIGH." Much better would cues like "BOTTOM CORNER" or "DRIVE LOW."

This is very important, because when your athlete tells himself NOT to do something, the focus becomes the very thing that he wants to avoid.

Try the following, first with yourself and then a variation for your athlete:

Whatever you do, in the next three seconds don't think of your athlete.

What is the first thing that you thought of? Probably your athlete. Why would you do that when the instruction was **not** to think of your athlete? It is because most of our instruction to you focused you on the very thing that you were to avoid thinking about.

The human mind cannot hold a negative. It can't, not think of something. In order not to think of something we have to first think of it! A more effective instruction not to think of your athlete would be to think of something else like "Think of your golf swing."

Think about how many times that coaches, parents, and athletes themselves lead into focusing on the very thing they are trying to ignore. "Don't choke," Don't worry about it," Don't get nervous," Don't let him get behind you," "Don't shank it," and on and on. Have your athlete always focus on what to do.

Negative Thought Stopping

No matter how proficient your athlete becomes in using sport psychology mental toughness techniques, it is likely that negative thoughts will still occur from time to time. There is a very simple, but effective, way to manage such negative thought episodes.

Negative Thought Stopping is a technique that can be used to control negative thinking. Developed by psychologist Dr. Joseph Cautela, it can be effectively used to clear interfering and distracting negative thoughts or images that intrude on your athlete's focus during competition. It can be used along with Attention Control Training to help your athlete return to an effective focus to performance whenever it is necessary to do so.

In our trainings, we usually show athletes how effective negative thought stopping can be in the following manner. We ask the athletes to close their eyes, sit quietly, and think a negative thought related to their performance. Then without warning, one of us will slam our hand on a table and yell **"STOP IT."**

Needless to say, the startled athletes sit bolt upright and their eyes pop wide open. But when asked whether the negative thought is still in their minds, the answer is always "No." They have been distracted away from the negative thinking.

You can either try this demonstration yourself with your athlete (assuming he or she is heart healthy) or you can simply explain the technique as it describe below.

HOW TO DO THE NEGATIVE THOUGHT STOPPING TECHNIQUE

> **SCAN YOUR THINKING AND SELF-TALK FOR ANY NEGATIVE THOUGHTS**

> **IF YOU FIND SOME:**
> **YELL (TO YOURSELF) THE WORDS "NO" OR "STOP IT"**

> **THEN GIVE YOURSELF A SKILL ORIENTED CUE WORD:**
> **USE WORDS LIKE *FOCUS, DRIVE IT, RELEASE, SMOOTH***
> *(Use a word related to your specific sport)*

> **EXECUTE THE SKILL AND FOCUS YOUR ATTENTION ON YOUR EVENT**

Again, this is a simple, but surprisingly powerful technique. Whenever your athlete becomes aware of a negative thought, tell him to FORCEFULLY think, say or "yell" (not out loud but in thought) the words NO or STOP IT. (Yelling "Stop It" out loud is just for the purpose demonstration. Athletes should "yell" internally to themselves and not out loud!) Then have your athlete immediately replace the negative thought with a skill-oriented cue word related to his sport like those mentioned above, or those used to psych up or STEP-UP, such as *STEADY, CHILL OUT, BACK TO IT, PUSH, or ACCELERATE, etc.*

The use of reorienting cues or commands like "Steady," "Accelerate," or even "Focus" after thought stopping is essential for effectiveness. Wegner (1989) has contributed much to our understanding of what makes the control of thinking effective. He reports that just trying to "directly suppress" a thought is not very effective, as it is much like trying to "not think of your athlete." Remember, the human mind is not built to "not think of something."

In fact, trying to directly suppress a thought can cause us to focus on it even more. There may also be a "rebound effect" in which we think about the banished thought even more frequently when the suppression attempt is stopped. If we are not effective in suppressing the thought, there may be an "intrusion reaction" where the thought recurs, and brings with it a strong emotional response (usually negative). Further, trying to just suppress a thought may not alter our body's reaction to it (again, usually negative stress-type reactions).

The use of negative thought stopping and distraction is much more effective. Distraction is thinking about something else, or replacing the unwanted thought with another thought or multiple thoughts. A single thought or multiple thoughts can be used as distracters (in fact, most people distract by using more than one thought). This will work best when the distracting thoughts are "absorbing," or of great interest and significance to your athlete. This is why SSST and STEPPIN-UP works so well. Having considered, planned, developed, and practiced distracting thoughts/self-statements prior to needing them will make them more effective.

Think positive. Be happy. But for maximum performance focus on SKILL SPECIFIC SELF-TALK.

X
THE FINAL WHISTLE:
AFFIRMATIONS, ATTITUDE
&
PUTTING IT ALL TOGETHER

Go out that door to victory!

-Knute Rockne
Legendary Notre Dame Football Coach
5 National Championships
5 Undefeated Seasons
Popularized the forward pass
"America's Most Reknowned Coach"

AFFIRMATIONS

There is one other approach to maximizing performance that is worth discussing briefly. This is the use of **AFFIRMATIONS** or positive thoughts and statements about oneself and one's abilities.

We are a bit ambivalent in suggesting affirmations, because caution is necessary in using "positive thinking" because while there may be some effect on attitude and motivation, this does not provide direction on *how* to maximize performance. We believe that a problem-solving, skill-oriented focus is the best mindset.

However, there is now some research that suggests that affirmations can reduce the body's physical response to stressful situations (Sherman et al., 2009). Further, since affirmations and positive statements can affect motivation, are commonly offered as a way to foster the winning attitude that is part of mental toughness, and because all athletes are different in what works for them, affirmations are worth discussing and using, at least as a secondary technique.

Affirmations are positive statements that athletes make to themselves about their personal characteristics, traits, and skills. They are not boasts or hopes. They are statements that remind your athlete of her strengths, talents, skills and goals. Affirmations work best when they are in the form of an "I" statement. They are also most effective when stated in the present tense. Affirmations are designed to be reviewed, stated, or meditated upon on a daily basis. They may have a role in critical situations, as well. And as noted above, they must be truthful, and not trash talk or boasts which could create unrealistic expectations.

There are two typical categories of affirmations. **PERSONAL AFFIRMATIONS** are statements that recognize your athlete's unique qualities. Personal affirmations might be:

I trust myself.

I feel good about my commitment to excellence.

I am a dedicated athlete.

My Team demonstrates readiness and determination.

PERFORMANCE AFFIRMATIONS are statements that recognize unique aspects of your athlete's skills and performance efforts. Performance affirmations might be:

I take pride in my preparation.

I strive for my personal best at all times.

I always work hard in practice

I strive to be a good teammate.

It would be helpful to have your athlete develop her own set of affirmations. If an affirmation represents a goal, or something that your athlete is working towards but has not yet achieved, it can be stated in the future tense rather than present tense. Such as rather than saying "I trust myself" the affirmation could be "I will learn to trust myself." Use the guides below to develop affirmations.

MY PERSONAL AFFIRMATIONS

_____

_____

_____

MY PERFORMANCE AFFIRMATIONS

_____

_____

_____

PUTTING IT ALL TOGETHER

You and your athlete now have a good basic awareness and understanding of the sport psychology skills that comprise mental toughness and maximize performance. It is up to your athlete to practice, develop, and utilize the skills that work best for her. One final way to help your athlete do this is to have her develop and use an extension of the psychological warm-up we discussed earlier; that is to develop a structured **Pre-Competition Psychological Warm-Up Routine.**

While mental toughness is maintained throughout the game or competition, and while it may be called upon at certain critical moments, a mental toughness mindset is initiated and bolstered by engaging in a pre-competition psychological warm-up routine.

Elite athletes prepare psychologically before each contest. They don't just arrive at the stadium, arena, track, or court and float out to compete with whatever mood or mindset they happen to be in that day. They prepare themselves psychologically, as well as, physically.

We are reminded of an elite professional soccer player, who was one of the nicest and helpful people you could ever meet, but there was always a point in the locker room before the game when he would sit on the bench, put on his earphones, and begin to focus. Woe to anyone who would interrupt this routine. When he looked up and removed his earphones it was clear that a transformation to readiness had occurred. You could see in his eye that "it was on." For the next two hours he would maintain a physical and psychological intensity that would overwhelm the opponents.

The following is an outline to help your athlete begin to develop a pre-competition psychological warm-up routine. Now that many different skills have been described for self-regulating up or down, they can begin to be applied in a routine for preparing to produce maximal performance every time. Your athlete doesn't have to follow the outline exactly. It is there, as is the sample routine, simply to give some guidance. It is followed by a sample psychological warm-up routine for a soccer player; again just as a guide. Your athlete should adapt and customize an approach that feels right to her, and remember that professional advice from coach, athletic trainer, sports medicine doc, or sport psychologist can always be a good idea to enhance the skills and routine.

On the next page, have your athlete fill in the sport psychology techniques that she will use to prepare mentally to maximize competitive performance.

MY PRE-COMPETITION PSYCHOLOGICAL WARM-UP ROUTINE

THE NIGHT BEFORE THE COMPETITION

_____
_____
_____

THE MORNING OF THE COMPETITION

_____
_____
_____

ON THE WAY TO THE COMPETITION

_____
_____
_____

IN THE LOCKER ROOM OR WHEN GETTING CHANGED

_____
_____
_____

DURING WARM-UPS

_____
_____
_____

AFTER THE COMPETITION

_____
_____
_____

OTHER SPECIAL COMPETITION SITUATIONS (Penalty kicks, free-throws, the long putt, field goal attempt, bases loaded, etc.)

_____
_____
_____

BEFORE PRACTICES

_____
_____
_____

EXAMPLE

PRE-COMPETITION PSYCHOLOGICAL WARM-UP ROUTINE

This is an example from a soccer player.

THE NIGHT BEFORE THE GAME

Image my plays for the game

Listen to mellow music to get to sleep

Eat right

THE MORNING OF THE COMPETITION

Review pointers from this week's practice and coach's suggestions

Read about an athlete that inspires me

ON THE WAY TO THE GAME

Final check of my gear

Review game strategy and what I know about the other team

Listen to music to get me pumped up (Queen's We are the Champions)

IN THE LOCKER ROOM OR WHEN GETTING CHANGED

Talk to my teammates and help them get into the game

Do my focus exercise

Get my game face on

DURING WARM-UPS

Do our warm-up drills

Image my body getting a controlled pump

Feel increasing power and quickness

Focus on my cue words: lightning, solid, on

AFTER THE GAME

Review stuff I did really well and also not as well as I wanted to do

Use imagery to correct any mistakes or poor moves I made

Talk to coach about my performance

OTHER SPECIAL GAME SITUATIONS

Penalty kick – focus my self-talk,

quick image of the target

attention control breath

BEFORE PRACTICES

Review my goals for today's practice

Image a skill before I work on it

Get psyched up for practice

A FINAL WORD(S) ON ATTITUDE

Self-talk, negative thought stopping, and affirmations intersect in the concept of **ATTITUDE.** They are the major ingredients in the quality of attitude. They provide the answer to HOW successful attitude is created and maintained. The essential role of attitude has been captured by Maxwell (2001):

ATTITUDE IS THE ADVANCE MAN OF OURSELVES.

ITS ROOTS ARE INWARD, BUT ITS FRUIT OUTWARD.
IT IS OUR BEST FRIEND AND OUR WORST ENEMY.
IT IS MORE HONEST AND MORE CONSISTENT THAN OUR WORDS.
IT IS AN OUTWARD LOOK BASED ON PAST EXPERIENCES.
IT IS A THING THAT DRAWS PEOPLE TO US OR REPELS THEM.
IT IS NEVER CONTENT UNTIL IT IS EXPRESSED.
IT IS THE LIBRARIAN OF OUR PAST.
IT IS THE SPEAKER OF OUR PRESENT.
IT IS THE PROPHET OF OUR FUTURE.

And also captured by elite professional soccer player:

I BELIEVE THAT ATTITUDE MORE THAN ANYTHING ELSE DETERMINES WHAT YOU WILL MAKE OF YOURSELF.

WE HAVE TO DREAM TO ACHIEVE HIGH GOALS ON THE PLAYING FIELD AND IN LIFE, BUT DREAMS CANNOT BECOME REALITY BY THEMSELVES. HARDWORK AND ATTITUDE WILL DETERMINE YOUR SUCCESS.

ATTITUDE IS NOT JUST HOW YOU SPEAK. IT IS HOW YOU WALK, WORK, PRESENT YOURSELF TO OTHERS, REACT TO SITUATIONS AND APPROACH LIFE. IT REFLECTS THE TRUE CORE OF WHO YOU ARE AND WHAT YOU BELIEVE.

ATTITUDE IS THE FOUNDATION ON WHICH YOU BUILD YOUR SPORTS SUCCESS AND YOUR PERSONAL ACCOMPLISHMENTS, YOUR RELATIONSHIPS WITH OTHERS AND THE QUALITY OF YOUR LIFE.

As they used to say in the '70's – "Shine On." May your athlete be driven by a full and healthy attitude, self-confidence, success with integrity, and mental toughness.

REFERENCES & RESOURCES

We have tried to introduce you and your athlete to the science and practice of sport psychology and mental toughness. This is just a start. As your athlete develops and progresses to higher levels of competition these concepts and skills will be even more important. What follows is a list of resources, some of which we used in writing this book, but also many others that you and your athlete may find helpful in striving for excellence in performance in sport and life.

> **It's what you learn after you know it all that counts.**
>
> **-John Wooden**
> UCLA Basketball
> The Wizard of Westwood

Beswick, B. 2nd ed. (2001). Focused for Soccer: Develop a Winning Mental Approach. Champaign, IL: Human Kinetics.

Burton, D. & Raedeke, T. (2008). Sport Psychology for Coaches. Champaign, IL: Human Kinetics.

Cohn, P. (1994). The Mental Game of Golf. South Bend, Indiana: Diamond Communications.

DeVito, C. (2001). The Ultimate Dictionary of Sports Quotations. New York: Checkmark Books.

Dorfman, H, & Kuehl, K. (1989). The Mental Game of Baseball: A Guide to Peak Performance. South Bend, Indiana: Diamond Communications.

Etnier, J. (2009). Bring Your "A" Game: Secrets for Training Your Brain for Success in Any Sport. Chapel Hill, NC: University of North Carolina Press.

Farley, K. & Curry, S. (1994). Get Motivated: Daily Psych-Ups. NY: Fireside.

Ferrell, M., Beach, R., Szeverneyi, N. (2006). An fMRI analysis of neural activity during perceived zone state performance. Journal of Sport and Exercise Psychology, 28, 421-433.

Hale, B., & Collins, D. (2002). Rugby Tough. Champaign, IL: Human Kinetics.

Harris, D., & Harris, B. (1984). Sports Psychology: Mental Skills for Physical People. NY: Leisure Press.

Loudis, L., Lobitz, W., & Singer, K. (1986). Skiing Out of Your Mind: The Psychology of Peak Performance. Champaign, IL: Human Kinetics.

Loehr, J. (1982), Mental Toughness Training for Sports. Lexington, MA: Stephen Green Press.

Lynberg, M. (1993). Winning: Great Coaches and Athletes Share their Secrets of Success. NY: Doubleday.

Lynch, J., & Scott, W. (1999). Running Within. Champaign, IL: Human Kinetics.

Martens, R. (1978).Joy and Sadness in Children's Sports. Champaign, Il: Human Kinetics.

May, J., & Asken, M. (1987). Sport Psychology: The Psychological Health of the Athlete. New York: PMA Publishing.

Mikes, J. (1987). Basketball FundaMENTALS: A Complete Mental Training Guide. Champaign, IL: Human Kinetics.

Miller, S. (2003). Hockey Tough. Champaign, IL: Human Kinetics.

Morris, T., Spittle, M., & Watt, A. (2005). Imagery in Sport. Champaign, Ill: Human Kinetics.

Murphy, S. (2005). Imagery: Inner Theater becomes reality. In S. Murphy (ed.) The Sport Psych Handbook. Champaign, Il: Human Kinetics.

Murphy, S. (1999). The Cheers and the Tears: A Healthy alternative to the Dark Side of Youth Sports Today. Jossey Bass.

Nelson, L. (1987), Sport Psychology: The Athlete's Perspective. In J. May & M. Asken, (Eds.) Sport Psychology: The Psychological Health of the Athlete. New York: PMA Publishing.

Nideffer, R, (1992). Psyched to Win. Champaign, Il: Human Kinetics.

Nideffer, R. (1985), Athletes' Guide to Mental Training. Champaign, IL: Human Kinetics.

Nideffer, R., & Sharpe, R. (1978), Attention Control Training: How to Get Control of Your Mind Through Total Concentration. New York: Wideview Books.

Orlick, T. (1986), Psyching for Sport. Champaign, Il: Human Kinetics.

Orlick, T. 4th ed. (2008). In Pursuit of Excellence. Champaign IL: Human Kinetics.

Porter, K. (2003). The Mental Athlete. Champaign, IL: Human Kinetics.

Ryan, J. (2000). Little Girls in Pretty Boxes: The Making and Breaking of Elite Gymnasts and Figure Skaters. Boston: Grand Central Publishing.

Scott, M. & Pellicioni, L., Jr. (1982). Don't Choke: How Athletes Can Become Winners. Englewood Cliffs, NJ: Prentice-Hall.

Shelton, T. & Mahoney, M. (1978), The content and effect of "psyching up" strategies in weightlifters. Cognitive Therapy & Research, 2, 275-284.

Sherman, D., Bunyan, D., Cresswell, J. & Jaremka, L. (2009). Psychological vulnerability and stress: The effects of self-affirmation on sympathetic nervous system responses to naturalistic stressors. Health Psychology, 28, (5)554-562.

Solomon, G., & Becker, A. (2006). Focused for Fastpitch. Champaign, Il: Human Kinetics.

Sperber, M. (2001). Beer and Circus: How Big-time College Sports are Crippling Undergraduate Education. Holt Paperbacks

Ungerleider, S. (2005). Mental Training for Peak Performance. Rodale Press.

Van Raalte, J., & Silver-Bernstein, C. (1999). Sport Psychology Library: Tennis. Morgantown, WV: Fitness Information Technology, Inc.

Wegner, D. (1989). White Bears and Other Unwanted Thoughts. NY: Penguin

Weinberg, R. (1988). The Mental Advantage: Developing Your Psychological Skills in Tennis. Champaign, IL: Human Kinetics.

www.ZoneofExcellence.ca Dr. Terry Orlick

The Institute for the Study of Youth Sport. www.educ.msu.edu/ysi/

www.yesports.com. Dr. Frank Smoll & Dr. Ronald Smith, University of Washington

ABOUT THE AUTHORS

Michael J. Asken, Ph.D.

Mike holds a B.A. degree in Social & Behavioral Sciences from the Johns Hopkins University. He completed his doctoral degree in Clinical Psychology with a minor in Medical Psychology at West Virginia University. He is a Fellow of the Division of Exercise and Sport Psychology of the American Psychological Association.

Mike was co-chair for the US Olympic Committee's 1987 National Conference on Sport Psychology. He has been an invited reviewer for the journal The Sport Psychologist. He has published articles on sport psychology in The International Journal of Sport Psychology, Family Medicine, Sports 'n Spokes, The Sport Psychologist, and the Physician and Sports Medicine. He is the author of Dying to Win: Preventing Drug Abuse in Sport and is co-author of Sport Psychology: The Psychological Health of the Athlete. He taught sport psychology at Lebanon Valley College, where he was given the Nevelyn Knisley Award for inspired teaching.

Mike has worked with athletes on psychological performance enhancement at the youth, high school, collegiate and professional levels. He was the team sport psychologist for the Harrisburg Heat professional indoor soccer team and the Hershey Wildcats professional outdoor soccer team. He has also worked with physically disabled athletes and Special Olympics. He has provided training in sport psychology to various high schools, youth sports organizations and athletic training groups.

In his current position, Mike has provided training in psychological performance skills and mental toughness to groups such as the FBI, Pennsylvania State Police, National Tactical Officers' Association, NYPD, the U.S. Army War College and US Navy Seals.

Breton M. Asken

Breton has played competitive soccer since the age of five. He was also the place kicker for his high school football team during his senior year. He is currently a junior at the University of North Carolina at Chapel Hill, majoring in Exercise and Sport Science and in (Neuro) Psychology. He is pursuing his certification as an athletic trainer, and has worked with high school athletes and the UNC Football and Track teams. He has been significantly involved with the sports concussion program at UNC.

CONCENTRATION GRID

23	12	07	15	62	93	82	36	21	37
31	50	59	28	46	30	25	48	69	76
45	49	73	19	02	67	04	77	41	64
26	29	88	03	34	13	91	38	56	86
87	83	98	35	43	44	24	39	40	20
90	96	89	80	42	94	53	05	55	57
61	75	65	32	22	11	08	10	27	09
00	99	95	85	14	01	74	60	92	81
18	51	71	54	63	17	79	33	70	52
97	78	58	84	06	16	66	72	47	68

Made in the USA
San Bernardino, CA
02 December 2017